New Persian Cooking

New Persian Cooking

A FRESH APPROACH TO THE CLASSIC CUISINE OF IRAN

JILA DANA-HAERI *with*

SHAHRZAD GHORASHIAN

PHOTOGRAPHY *by* JASON LOWE

I.B. TAURIS

LONDON · NEW YORK

I would like to dedicate this book to the memory of my mother and to our cook, Gholam, who through his warmth and humour inspired my love of cooking.

JILA DANA-HAERI

Distributed in the United States and Canada Exclusively by
Palgrave Macmillan
175 Fifth Avenue, New York NY 10010

ISBN: 978 1 84885 586 1

A full CIP record for this book is available from the British Library
A full CIP record is available from the Library of Congress

Library of Congress Catalog Card Number: available

Typeset in RenardNo2 by www.rawshock.co.uk

Printed and bound in Italy by Printer Trento Srl.

MIX
Paper from responsible sources
FSC® C015829
www.fsc.org

Contents

Acknowledgements

This book would not have been possible without the tremendous support of our family and friends. Dori Dana-Haeri encouraged and supported us and held our hands throughout the process of creating this book; she negotiated and represented us, cracked the whip and organized us to cook, write and keep to deadlines. Without her this project would not have come to fruition.

Neda Dana-Haeri contributed recipes for some of the special dishes that she cooks for family get-togethers. In her quiet way, Neda has always been there, helping us cook and prepare for photo shoots.

John Bateson tested the recipes as a newcomer to Persian cooking and also contributed his ice cream recipes inspired by Persian ingredients. We found his comments invaluable in making the recipes more user-friendly. Jacque Thomson also tested recipes and made helpful comments.

Jason Lowe's positive energy, love of Persian food and culture, has brought these recipes to life through his beautiful pictures.

Last but not least we thank the I.B.Tauris editorial team for their hard work, and valuable advice in guiding us throughout the process of getting the book ready for publication.

Preface

I grew up with the tastes and aromas of Persian cuisine all around me. My mother was an excellent cook: she loved to entertain, and her delicious food created many memorable occasions. The ritual of preparing, serving and eating good food was very important in our household. Since moving to England in the 1980s I have tried to recreate a similar atmosphere in my kitchen and to celebrate this aspect of my culture. *New Persian Cooking* is the result of many years of exploring and adapting recipes, replacing ingredients and coming up with new ideas in the hope of bringing the richness and variety of Persian cuisine to enthusiasts in search of new tastes.

My aim is to make Persian recipes accessible to a wider audience, using readily available ingredients and simpler, less time-consuming methods of cooking. For example, in my recipes for *aashes* – thick, hearty soups with many variations – I have replaced lamb meat, which is traditionally used in *aashes*, with chicken or vegetable stock. This means that the recipe takes less time to cook and is lighter and more acceptable to a Western palate. I have also included several methods of cooking rice, from the elaborate and time-consuming to simpler and quicker versions. Some rice dishes are traditionally cooked with the meat embedded in the rice. My versions allow for cooking the meat separately and adding it as the dish is being arranged on the serving platter – so almost all the rice recipes can be prepared as vegetarian dishes.

I was brought up in the southern Iranian city of Shiraz but, as my mother came from Bushehr on the Persian Gulf, we spent our holidays at my grandfather's house there. It was a magical place, and the intensity, the brightness and the warmth of the sun is etched forever on my memory. It is as though the sun always shone on the massive red bougainvillaea covering the beautiful balcony of my grandfather's house. I roamed around in the big old house and wandered through wild gardens dotted with separate buildings in the vast and secure space I called home.

In the evenings, when the sun's rays left the garden and the gardeners began watering the plants, the smell of water on parched earth filled the air, signalling the return of the adults and the family gathering for the evening meal. Each member of the family was greeted with an ice-cold glass of a home-made *sharbat* made from essences of orange blossom or other herbs or flowers, each with its own health-giving properties. I remember some with dread because, to my young palate, their taste seemed overwhelmingly medicinal! Others, however, I looked forward to drinking. My particular favourite, *Sharbat-e khiar sekanjabin* (p. 217), was a mixture of finely chopped cucumber in iced water, sweetened with a syrup made of sugar and vinegar. Complete with a sprig of fresh mint, this was paradise in a glass!

Even now, when I close my eyes and think of Bushehr, I can still vividly remember waking in the mornings to the smell of fresh bread. I remember the old lady who made bread in the clay oven in the garden of grandfather's house. From the veranda that surrounded the house, I used to watch the arrival of woven baskets containing fresh fish, herbs and all the ingredients for the meals of the day. My memories of the big kitchen in my grandfather's house are full of laughter and noise, the smells of rich spices and fragrant herbs and the enormous steaming pans on wood-burning stoves.

As a child in Shiraz, I always came home from school filled with anticipation. I would immediately go to the kitchen where Ghoolo (my name for our cook Gholam) would be waiting for me with a big smile and a bowl of home-made custard (in our house we called it crème anglaise). He would give me a little stool to stand on so I could reach the work surfaces and see what he was doing. At that time of the day Ghoolo was always busy preparing the dinner. He would explain what the meal was to be and would ask me to help him in small ways, telling me stories as he cooked. I remember feeling a part of the whole process and proud of being allowed to join in. The whole kitchen was filled with the aroma of onions frying and meat cooking. Depending on the menu, herbs or vegetables were chopped and added to the pot. And before you knew it, from the disparate contents of several pots, he would conjure up the most wonderful dishes. How I wished to be able, one day, to work my own magic and produce the same results as he did. Almost half a century later, as I cook in my own kitchen, his instructions echo in my head from time to time. I try to recreate the aroma, consistency and taste that he achieved.

We always celebrated Norouz, the Persian New Year – heralding the arrival of spring on 21 March – with pomp and ceremony. My mother was very particular about the Norouz festival and insisted on observing traditions and customs. Special cakes and sweets were baked several weeks beforehand, ready for the guests who arrived daily for the traditional exchange of New Year's greetings. Family members and friends would come to stay for the holiday, and the whole occasion was full of the hustle and bustle of cooking and festive food. On New Year's Eve we had sweet and colourful rice (*Morassa' polo*, p. 155) with saffron chicken (*Joojeh za'farani*, p. 97) or a lamb dish garnished with fried potatoes and nuts, known as *gheimeh* or *Khoresht-e gheimeh* (p. 77). On New Year's Day, fried fish with herb rice (*Sabzi polo*, p. 159), light and heady with the aroma of the herbs, seemed to offer all the promise of spring. Everyone wore new clothes – part of the tradition of greeting the New Year – and we children, oblivious to the hard work going on around us, paraded in our finery and enjoyed the gifts that we were given. It was customary for the grown-ups to give children crisp new banknotes or gold coins as New Year presents.

At the end of summer our house in Shiraz buzzed with food-related activities. We brought in extra help to prepare and conserve fruit, vegetables and herbs for the winter. Aubergines/eggplants, a popular ingredient in Persian cooking, were dried on the line in the sun before being pickled. Limes and lemons were pressed and the juice bottled. I remember the arrival of baskets full of lemons and limes, followed by the ritual of cutting them in half and squeezing them using a rolling pin on a big chopping board placed over a large bowl. The idea was to extract virtually all of the juice from several lemons simultaneously, with the husks discarded into another bowl. The juice was then bottled and kept in cool cellars, creating row after row of colourful bottles, rather like soldiers on a parade ground.

Another autumn ritual in Persian households was the preparation of tomato paste. Large quantities of ripe tomatoes were spread on clean sheets to dry partially in the sun. The tomatoes were then put through a special mill to extract their skins and pips; the resulting thick liquid was poured into shallow bowls and left in the sun to thicken further. (You could cheat slightly and let the tomato juice simmer gently instead of leaving it in the sun. This would speed up the process, but strict followers of the traditional method would say that the taste was not the same.) Once the correct consistency was achieved, the paste would be poured into sterilized jars and stored in a cool place, usually the cellar, for use throughout the year. During the preparation period, the whole house smelt of tomatoes. For the children, it was a treat to be allowed to help. Sometimes the tomatoes were put in big pans before being put through the mill, and we were recruited to stamp on them to help separate the skins. (Needless to say, our feet and legs were thoroughly washed beforehand.) This was a very enjoyable exercise which we eagerly looked forward to – and which inevitably led to chaos and unruly behaviour!

These days, even in Iran, few people observe those rituals – almost everything is now available all year round in supermarkets. But the romance of the process is gone and, with the industrial production methods that have taken over, much of the original delicacy of taste has disappeared.

Street vendors also herald the changing seasons in Iran. With the chill autumn air comes the warmth and aroma of vegetables cooked and sold on the streets. Broad beans/fava beans, boiled in their pods in salt water (*Baghala pokhteh*), are served straight from the steaming pot, sprinkled with *golpar*, a spice made from the ground seeds of a native Persian plant, to enhance the flavour. The result is simply delicious.

Deeper into the winter, as colder weather brings the threat of snow, other national favourites hit the streets. Boiled beetroot, *laboo*, glistening red, sweet and hot, bought for a few pennies and eaten on the way home from school, was a nutritious treat that more than made up for the weather. Boiled turnip, *shalgham*, renowned for its healing and soothing properties, was also on offer – but not for the faint-hearted! As children we preferred colourful and sweet *laboo* to the stronger flavour of *shalgham*.

As spring blossoms appeared on fruit trees, the promise of sour greengages and newly formed almond buds, picked before the inner skin had a chance to harden, made our mouths water. On roadsides, balanced on rickety stools, shiny round trays held mounds of the freshly picked fruit. This was some time before the greengages appeared in grocery stores or supermarkets, and when they did, they never tasted as good.

Later on in the year a wealth of swollen, juicy mulberries would be heaped on the same trays, delicately arranged in ever-decreasing circles ending in a proud point. We would buy a dozen or so and savour the intensely sweet and subtly perfumed fruit, making each one last as long as possible.

Towards the end of the summer, as the evenings became cooler, small braziers full of smouldering lumps of charcoal joined the stools and trays. On these, corn on the cob was roasted to perfection. Fussy customers insisted on choosing their own cob. It was roasted on the fire, then swiftly dunked in a bucket of salted water to cool down and season the cob, before being offered to the customer.

About the same time of year, fresh walnuts found their way to the street vendors' trays. Each nut was carefully shelled and the inner light brown skin was peeled off, revealing the gleaming white fruit. The trick was to keep the nut whole, because only the whole nut would be good enough to sell. A small pyramid made of four walnuts was the unit for sale, a *faal*. As the *faals* were sold new ones replaced them, fished out of a bucket of salted water. In between serving customers the vendor continued to shell and peel walnuts, dropping them into the bucket.

Street food intrigued us; it signalled the seasons of the year. We learnt to anticipate certain seasonal dishes at home according to what was on offer in the streets. For example, when we saw the mounds of broad beans cooked in their pods being sold on the roadsides, we knew that Ghoolo would soon be serving up *Baghala polo* (p. 141) at home.

All through my childhood and adolescent years I was interested in cooking as a creative process, seeing raw ingredients turned into plates of delicious food. By far the greatest influence on my cooking was my mother. She was a consummate host and her dinner parties were the talk of Shiraz. At the table, food was savoured in small servings accompanied by lively conversation. She used the best ingredients and paid attention to details: how the table was set, how the food was served and which food combinations went well together. My mother was famous for her inventive and unusual recipes, all rooted in basic Persian traditions. Her exacting standards still guide me in my cooking.

As a family we always ate together in the dining room. Meal times were important, and food played a significant part in our lives – a tradition that continued after we all left Iran. The weekends now are special family occasions. In the tranquil setting of the English countryside we try to recreate the atmosphere we grew up in, devoting care and attention to family meals.

Jila Dana-Haeri

THE BACKGROUND TO THIS BOOK

We have known each other since the late 1960s, when we were both at university in Shiraz, and we have shared many wonderful meals with each other's families and friends. The Persian dishes we served at these gatherings have received countless compliments both from those brought up with Persian cooking and others new to the experience. As the children of our generation grew up and began to have families of their own, they have asked us for recipes for Persian dishes. A book bringing those recipes together with tips and guidance on how to achieve results, we thought, would be the way to proceed. We knew that it would be a challenge, not least to pin down recipes that are prone to change from one use to the next: flavours can become more complex or simpler depending on the occasion, the season or the cook's mood.

We spent a summer at Shahrzad's house in the south of France to test the recipes. It proved a memorable time for both of us, a continuous feast of cooking, tasting and writing in Shahrzad's tiny kitchen.

As Shahrzad has been a vegetarian for many years, we cooked vegetarian versions of many recipes.

It was about this time that our photographer, Jason Lowe, contacted us out of the blue – a great stroke of luck for us. Jason had spent some time in Iran during his childhood and had fallen in love with Persian food.

Writing this book has been a true labour of love. We share with our families the Persian delight in poetry, wine and, of course, good food. As we worked on the book, many an evening was spent cooking, eating and chatting together until the small hours. We both find the world of food enormously relaxing and liberating – and choosing recipes is like entering a parallel universe of possibilities. We have relished all the different stages of putting this book together, and we hope you gain as much pleasure from cooking the recipes as we did in selecting them.

Jila Dana-Haeri and Shahrzad Ghorashian

Introduction

Persian cuisine is quite distinct from other 'Middle Eastern' styles of cooking in the way it emphasizes presentation, colour and fragrance. It combines herbs and spices with the main ingredients to create intriguing layers of flavour and aroma, none of which overwhelm the others. It is also healthy because it is based largely on using fresh ingredients at their seasonal peak, and does not rely heavily on meat: many of the recipes are suitable for vegetarians. It offers plenty of opportunity to be innovative with recipes, adapting them to the tastes of your family and guests.

Persia's geography, history and cultural influences have shaped the diversity of ingredients and the methods of cooking in one of the world's oldest and most sophisticated cultures. Persia – or Iran – has been subjected to repeated invasions, but it has maintained its culture, language and identity throughout the centuries. The vast size of the country encompasses a wide array of local dialects, lifestyles, regional traditions and customs, not to mention an extraordinary variety of landscapes and climates. All these are reflected in the country's food. In the north, around the southern coast of the Caspian Sea, the landscape is lush and green and as a result of plentiful rainfall there is great diversity of fruit, vegetables and herbs. The northern regional cuisine features simple, fresh notes of taste and aroma, and there is a preference for sweet and sour flavours, as opposed to spicy. Further south, in the provinces near the Persian Gulf, where the climate is drier, the season for fresh ingredients is much shorter and the variety available is not as great. There is also a long tradition of trade through the sea routes with spice-rich countries like India. The resulting cuisine is more complex in taste than in the north of the country, with long notes of spices, tamarind and chillies.

Visitors to Persian courts throughout the centuries have commented on the lavish feasts they experienced. Until the early twentieth century Iranian rooms were filled with colourful carpets, and it would be on these carpets that the meal would be laid out. With plenty of cushions for support, families gathered around the *sofreh*, a tablecloth spread on the carpet over a thick cover, often made of leather. Even today, in some households the tradition of *sofreh* is still alive. All the dishes – *aash* (soup), rice and *khoreshts* (dishes combining vegetables and meat in a rich sauce), fresh herbs and salads, bread and feta cheese – were set out on the *sofreh*. Everyone helped themselves and food could be eaten in any order. Tucking into little parcels of cheese and fresh herbs wrapped in a piece of bread made a fitting end to the meal. After the *sofreh* was cleared away, tea and home-made sweets would appear. Tea – never drunk with milk – was served in small, waisted glass tumblers that showed the rich amber colour of the drink. Sweets included *noghl* (sugar-coated almond sticks perfumed with orange blossom water or rose water), dates and baklava, among others.

Food has always been an important element in the Persian way of life. No one knows when or where the world's first cookbook was written, but history suggests that the Persians can stake a claim. We know that the armies of ancient Persia took their food seriously. In the wars between Greeks and Persians from the sixth to the fourth century BC, military cooks were expected to participate in the fighting. The more elevated cooks who catered for the king and his generals had to dictate their cooking procedures to soldiers or prisoners of war who were literate, so that even if the cooks were injured or killed during the day's fighting, their leaders' appetites could be satisfied in the evening.

The ancient Persians were great lovers of wine, and today the traditional Persian grape Shiraz (Syrah) is grown all over the world. The red wine it produces is a wonderful complement to many Persian dishes. Although wine drinking has been discouraged in Iran since the arrival of Islam in the seventh century, Iranians have continued to produce and drink wine through the centuries, with or without the approval of the authorities. Persian poetry is awash with references to wine and the joy of drinking, whether in the mystic sense or otherwise.

From grapes to wheat and rice, Iran's diverse climate, physical geography and terrain are ideal for growing a vast array of agricultural products. The land of Persia forms part of the fertile band that stretches from the foothills of the Himalayas to the western coast of the Black Sea. Bordered by the Caspian Sea to the north and the Persian Gulf to the south, the Zagros mountain chain dominates the west of the country. Especially on the Caspian lowlands and well-watered Elburz mountains in northern Iran, fruit and vegetables are particularly tasty; dairy products, enjoying the same conditions, are also exceptionally good. Many native Persian plants, such as pomegranates, saffron, pistachios and various herbs, bring their own unique colours and flavours. Persian cuisine has used the natural advantages of high-quality, fresh ingredients to develop some exquisitely subtle but complex tastes.

Lamb is the meat traditionally used in Persian cooking. However, in recent times beef has replaced lamb in some dishes. Chicken has always been very popular and widely used. Game birds are eaten as seasonal delicacies. The varieties of fish available in the Caspian Sea in the north and the Persian Gulf in the south are very different and regional recipes have developed in coastal areas.

Seasonal variation – many parts of Iran have cold winters and very hot summers – has always shaped the nature and diversity of Persian cooking. Globalization and the flow of worldwide trade have to some extent reduced the seasonality of ingredients, but traditionally, as different ingredients appear in the marketplace throughout the year, seasonal change is reflected in popular recipes. Okra and lamb *khoresht* (*Khoresht-e bamiyeh*, p. 68) and broad beans and dill rice

(*Baghala polo*, p. 141) are just two examples.

The combination of fresh and cooked food eaten over the course of a day has a good nutritional balance. A traditional Persian table offers combination of proteins from animal and plant sources – the healthiest way to meet your body's protein requirements. A side dish of yogurt, mixed with cucumbers and mint or beetroot or celery, has many nutritional benefits, while a fresh bouquet of herbs provides enough vitamins and antioxidants to boost your immune system on a daily basis. Fruit, rich in vitamins and fibre, is the most popular end to a rich meal. On hot summer days slices of ruby-coloured watermelon and sweet chilled rock melon (*kharbozeh*) are much in demand. A large bowl of colourful seasonal fruit adorns the coffee tables of most households in Iran.

Modern Persian cooking reflects its varied heritage, but has also evolved to encompass trends in healthy eating. Drawing on the tradition of serving fresh herbs and yogurt with meals, salads and yogurt side dishes are important features of today's dinner table. The move away from animal fats to vegetable oils is a relatively recent major change in Persian kitchens. Modern cooking puts more emphasis on baking and grilling meat and vegetables, wherever possible, rather than frying them.

SPECIAL FEATURES OF PERSIAN CUISINE

Presentation is an important aspect of Persian cooking, and nowhere is this more evident than in the country's famous rice dishes. Great attention is paid to the preparation and presentation of rice dishes, each of which offers a unique taste and range of colours. A dish of rice should delight the eye with its colourful beauty as well as exciting the appetite with its aroma. Even plain rice is decorated with saffron to give it visual impact. The beauty of broad beans and dill rice (*Baghala polo*, p. 141), for example, lies in the contrast between the bright green crescents of fresh broad beans, the faintly saffroned yellow grains of rice and the dark green strands of fresh dill. Saffron jewelled rice *(Morassa' polo* or *Shirin polo*, p. 155), colourful, decorative and perfumed, is a 'must' for celebrations such as weddings, offering a feast for the eye as well as the palate. A large tray of saffron-coloured rice, with its gleaming and colourful pieces of candied orange peel, pistachio and almond slivers, is festive in every sense of the word. In fact the more festive the occasion, the more elaborately prepared and decorated the dish.

Fresh bread is an important part of any Persian meal. Among many delicious varieties, you will find *lavash* (paper-thin round bread), *taaftoon* (thin flat bread), *barbari* (thick flat bread) and *sangak* (wholemeal bread made in clay ovens on a bed of hot gravel). Freshly baked bread is traditionally bought just before each meal in Iran, and served still warm from the oven. Its aroma was so irresistible that as children we would surreptitiously help ourselves from the kitchen, in spite of protests that we would ruin our appetites. Sometimes we devoured so much that a second trip to the baker's was required!

Unexpected flavours are keynotes of Persian cuisine. However, the aim is to achieve layers of subtle tastes and flavours. For example, the tangy flavour of aubergine and lamb *khoresht* (*Khoresht-e badenjan*, p. 65), using verjuice as a seasoning, is markedly different from that of lamb and potato *khoresht* (*Khoresht-e seebzamini*, p. 85) in which tamarind is used for the same purpose. Lime juice, lemon juice and sumac are among other tangy, mouthwatering ingredients widely used in Persian cooking.

Rose water and dried rose petals are often used to flavour and decorate dishes. The most famous areas for the production of rose water are villages around Kashan, Qamsar and Niasar, in the centre of Iran, although as a child I also remember seeing mounds of rose buds piled up in gardens along the banks of the Dry River in Shiraz.

The elegant, single-layered rose that grows in the fields of Qamsar has an exquisite perfume, and it is cultivated solely for its scent. Packets of rose petals and bottles of rose water are sold in Middle Eastern shops in the West.

Fragrances, flavours, sounds and colours seem to have a unique intensity in Iran. On market stalls, the vibrant colours of turmeric, sumac, *zereshk* and pomegranate dazzle the eye. In the chaotic labyrinths of bazaars you will encounter a complex range of aromas, from saffron to cardamom, rose water to orange blossoms, all bringing inspiration to the country's cuisine.

HOW TO USE THIS BOOK

To make Persian cooking more accessible to Western cooks, we have begun each chapter with a general introduction to styles and cooking methods. Careful preparation and gentle simmering are key to many Persian dishes. In order to make planning easier, we have separated the preparation from the actual cooking, and given approximate times for each. Wherever possible, we have indicated when preparation and/or cooking can be done in advance. Tips for achieving better results have been included in the recipes where relevant. Some ingredients will be new to those trying Persian cooking for the first time, and we look at these in detail in Chapter 1. We strongly recommend reading this chapter and the introductory information before attempting any of the dishes.

However, don't be afraid to be guided by your taste buds, as every Persian cook is. Once you have tried a recipe, you can make it your own by adjusting the ingredients to your taste. For example, many of the dishes in the book can be cooked without meat to suit vegetarians, and we have indicated these where relevant.

CHAPTER 1 features some ingredients that are unfamiliar to cooks in other countries. Persian Essentials explores these ingredients and gives advice on how to obtain, store and use them.

CHAPTER 2 includes recipes for *aash* (the traditional Persian thick soup) and other soups, which we have modified to a certain extent for Western cooks. Most *aashes* can be served either as a first course or a main course and almost all can be made without meat.

CHAPTER 3 consists of recipes for *khoreshts* (a typical Persian dish with plenty of sauce, always served with plain white rice). We have adapted some of Iran's most popular recipes, which draw on a range of pulses, vegetables and herbs, plus meat if desired, to create tasty and nutritious meals.

CHAPTER 4 offers recipes for *khoraks*, *kababs*, *kooftehs* and other main meals that have very little or no sauce, and are often served with potatoes or bread rather than rice. We have collected some variations on well-known Persian dishes, including meat, poultry, fish and vegetarian dishes.

CHAPTER 5 illustrates the diversity of Persian rice dishes. It explains the different methods of preparing and cooking rice that characterize Persian cuisine, including the delicious *tahdig* (the crispy layer that forms at the bottom of the pan as the rice cooks). Some recipes are complete meals in their own right – many of them vegetarian – while others provide tasty accompaniments to meat, poultry or fish dishes.

CHAPTER 6 includes recipes for salads and side dishes, some of which can also be served as first courses in a Western-style menu. There are delicious yogurt dishes, light herby salads and unusual combinations of fruits and leaves.

Persian cuisine places little emphasis on desserts. Ice creams and sorbets are popular but they are usually eaten as snacks in the afternoon or summer evenings rather than at the end of a meal.

CHAPTER 7 offers Persian-style sweet dishes that can function as desserts within a Western menu.

CHAPTER 8 is an introduction to a number of popular cold and hot drinks served in Iran. Some are based on essences of herbs and flowers, which are believed to have medicinal properties.

The majority of the recipes in this book use simple, fresh ingredients that are readily available from food markets and supermarkets throughout the world. Just a handful of items, such as dried limes or rose petals, may require seeking out in Middle Eastern shops or online. In celebrating Persian cuisine, we hope this book brings its culinary delights to a wider audience.

Happy cooking!

Conversions and Equivalents

UK/US terms

Aubergine/eggplant

Beetroot/beets

Bicarbonate of soda/baking soda

Broad beans/fava beans

Caster sugar/superfine sugar

Chicory/Belgian endive

Cling film/plastic wrap

Coriander/cilantro (fresh coriander)

Cornflour/cornstarch

Courgette/zucchini

Double cream/heavy cream

Frying pan/skillet

Full-fat (e.g. milk, yogurt) /whole milk

Gherkin/cornichon

Grill/broil

Icing sugar/confectioners' sugar

Lamb's lettuce/corn salad

Mangetout/snow peas

Minced/ground (meat)

Muslin/cheesecloth

Plain flour/all-purpose flour

Prawn/shrimp

Rocket/arugula

Single cream/light cream

Spring onions/scallions

Stoned/pitted

Sultana/golden raisin

Tahini/sesame paste

Tomato purée/tomato paste

Measurements

The measurements given within the recipes should be treated as guidelines, the best measurement of all being personal taste.

Weight measurements are provided in imperial and metric. These correspond closely with US measurements, e.g. 1 oz equals approximately 30 g.

For liquid measurements the simplest conversion to US equivalents is:

IMPERIAL	METRIC	AMERICAN
$\frac{1}{2}$ fluid oz	15 ml	1 tablespoon
8 fl oz	225 ml	1 cup
10 fl oz ($\frac{1}{2}$ pint)	300 ml	$1\frac{1}{4}$ cups
16 fl oz	450 ml	2 cups (1 US pint)
20 fl oz (1 pint)	570 ml	$2\frac{1}{2}$ cups ($1\frac{1}{4}$ US pints)
30 fl oz ($1\frac{1}{2}$ pints)	850 ml	$3\frac{3}{4}$ cups
40 fl oz (2 pints)	1.2 litres	5 cups

The following weight-to-cup conversion table is a rough approximation only:

IMPERIAL	METRIC	AMERICAN
2 oz	50 g	$\frac{1}{4}$ cup
4 oz	120 g	$\frac{1}{2}$ cup
8 oz	225 g	1 cup
16 oz	450 g	2 cups

Chapter 1

PERSIAN ESSENTIALS

Chapter 1

Persian essentials

OPPOSITE

Fresh rose petals.

S mell can conjure up memories more potently than any other sense. And through memory we relive experiences. At least this holds true for me. Unscrew a jar of turmeric and I am back as a child in the kitchen of our house in sleepy 1960s Shiraz in southern Iran, celebrated as a city of poetry and mirth. Even as a young child I was bewitched by the flavours and aromas emanating from our family kitchen.

The visual appeal of a Persian spread is as important as the aroma and taste of the food. A platter of rice will be decorated with an elaborate garnish or drizzled with saffron to add colour to the fluffy white grains. To give another example, *Aash-e maast* (p. 45) is a simple hearty soup based on the subtle flavours of pulses and herbs, enriched by the addition of yogurt. The garnish of fried onions and garlic includes dried mint for colour, aroma and flavour, hitting high notes of taste that contrast with the deep warmth of the *aash*. The garnish also adds visual impact to the light green soup.

Many of the ingredients used in Persian dishes are familiar throughout the world, such as lemon juice, tomato purée/ tomato paste, pulses and a great variety of spices and herbs, both fresh and dried. However, to create the exquisite tastes and textures of Persian cooking you will need a number of exotic ingredients: saffron, pomegranate, rose petals, barberries and dried limes are among the more unusual. Nowadays,

supermarkets in the West stock many of these ingredients. Middle Eastern and Mediterranean stores are likely sources of special Persian spices, herbs and dried fruits. Most of the dry ingredients keep for a reasonable period of time, so you can buy them when you come across them and store them until needed.

A well-stocked store cupboard provides flexibility and spontaneity for any style of cooking, and Persian cooking is no exception: with a few essentials sitting in your cupboard, you can prepare a range of dishes with little pre-planning.

Some Persian dishes are quicker to make than others. Many recipes – for example most *khoreshts*, *khoraks* and *aashes* – involve long, slow cooking, but you can usually prepare them in advance and then reheat them and garnish them before serving the following day. In some cases this improves the taste and texture of the dish.

Whether you choose the simplest or the most elaborate recipes, with the right ingredients to hand and a little forward planning, you will be able to impress your family and friends with delicious flavours, and without a last-minute rush.

In this chapter, I have sought to gather together the spices and staples that define Persian cuisine.

✻

Aubergine/eggplant
(Badenjan)

Aubergines/eggplants are often used in Persian cooking and aubergines are described by Persians as 'meat for the poor'. They are used in a variety of ways: smoked and mashed with egg; fried with tomatoes and mushrooms; fried, mashed and mixed with yogurt or *kashk*; or pickled. Aubergine and lamb *khoresht* (*Khoresht-e badenjan*, p. 65) is a very popular traditional dish in which sliced aubergine is cooked in a casserole with tender lamb. Aubergine is also used for making stuffed vegetables (*Dolmeh*, p. 119). There are several different varieties of aubergine: the thin, long variety is better for a *khoresht*, while the shorter, rounder type is preferable for stuffing, although in the West you are unlikely to have much choice and the varieties are interchangeable in most Persian recipes.

Above: A tribal woman making butter from diluted yogurt in the traditional way. See p. 22 for oils and cooking fats.

Storage

Choose firm, unwrinkled aubergines with tight, shiny skin; store in the fridge for up to a week.

Preparation

Wash and dry the aubergine and cut off the green stem at the top. If the recipe calls for the aubergine to be peeled, use a vegetable peeler to remove the purple skin.

Barberry
(*Zereshk*)

Barberries are the bright red fruit of a thorny shrub (*Berberis vulgaris*); they have been used medicinally for more than 2,500 years. In the Persian kitchen they are generally used dried, but they retain their colour, and the ruby red, almost translucent berries decorate a number of traditional dishes. They are best known as an ingredient of a sweet and sour rice dish, *Zereshk polo* (p. 164). *Zereshk* is sold in sachets in Mediterranean and Middle Eastern shops.

Storage

Store the sachet in the fridge. After the sachet is opened, *zereshk* will keep for a good few weeks in the fridge or a couple of months in the freezer.

Preparation

Measure out the amount required for the recipe. Spread the berries on a tray and discard any that are discoloured and any stalks that remain on the fruit. Wash and drain several times, then soak in a bowl of cold water for 10–15 minutes before using.

Cucumbers, Middle Eastern variety
(*Khiar*)

Persian or Middle Eastern cucumbers are slender and usually no more than 15 cm/6 inches long. They are significantly more

OPPOSITE

Dried barberries.

aromatic and crunchy than other varieties – you often see them in Persian fruit bowls! They are also served lightly salted, as a snack. Small cucumbers are particularly tasty in salads and yogurt mixtures, and in summer drinks. You can buy them from Middle Eastern shops and some supermarkets; if you cannot find the Persian variety, choose small cucumbers, which will have a more delicate flavour and fewer seeds.

Storage

Whichever variety or size, choose firm, weighty cucumbers. Wash and dry the cucumbers, wrap them in a clean tea towel, and store in the fridge for up to a week.

Preparation

Depending on the recipe you can peel, slice, chop or grate the cucumbers. In some recipes they are not peeled before use.

Fenugreek
(Shambaleeleh)

This is a plant native to the eastern Mediterranean region; it is also found in India, where it is known as *methi*. Many health benefits are attributed to fenugreek, including lowering cholesterol, helping diabetes sufferers, reducing hair loss and increasing the milk supply in lactating mothers.

Fenugreek leaves are used as a herb, both fresh and dried, and the seeds are ground as a spice. In Persian cooking the leaves are used more often than the seeds, although the seeds are sometimes used in pickles. I prefer dried fenugreek because of its stronger, more intense aroma in dishes such as the traditional soup, *Eshkeneh* (p. 52); a popular lamb and bean casserole, *Khoresht-e ghormeh sabzi* (p. 79) owes its distinctive aroma and flavour to this herb. Sachets of dried fenugreek are sold in Mediterranean and Middle Eastern shops.

Storage

Store dried fenugreek in a cool, dark place; after the sachet is opened the fenugreek will keep for about a month.

Store fresh fenugreek as other fresh herbs (p. 18).

Preparation

When using dried leaves, soak them in cold water, in a small bowl, for up to an hour. Drain in a colander before use.

Golpar

Literally meaning the 'wing of a flower', *golpar* (*Heracleum persicum* or Persian hogweed) grows wild in the mountainous regions of Iran. The ground seedpods are used as a spice, aromatic and tasty, sprinkled on snacks and vegetable dishes such as cooked broad beans/fava beans, and on fresh fruit, such as pomegranate seeds. *Golpar* is sold in sachets in Middle Eastern shops; sometimes referred to, erroneously, as angelica seeds.

Storage

Golpar loses its aroma quite quickly, so use it within a few weeks of buying it. Store in a cool, dark place. Once you have opened the sachet, keep the powder in an airtight jar.

Herbs

Persian cooking makes great use of fresh herbs in season. Some are eaten raw in starters, salads and side dishes, others are cooked in soups and main courses. Fresh herbs are delicious (and easily available) during the spring and summer, when one craves lighter tastes. *Sabzi khordan*, a dish of fresh mint, basil, tarragon, chives, summer savory and watercress, is the usual accompaniment to Persian meals throughout the spring and summer. Served with a block of shimmering white sheep's milk cheese – feta is the nearest equivalent in the West – *Sabzi khordan* makes a perfect appetizer.

In the cold winter months, the more concentrated aroma of dried herbs complements the flavour of *aashes* (thick soups) and rich main dishes. Almost all dishes that use fresh herbs in their preparation can also be made with dried herbs, although there is of course some difference in taste.

The most commonly used herbs are almost all available in the West in both dried and fresh forms. They include basil, chives, coriander/cilantro, dill, *marzeh* (summer savory), mint, oregano, parsley (usually the flat-leafed variety), spring onions/scallions, tarragon and watercress.

Storage

Fresh herbs can be kept for up to a week. The secret is to wash and dry them and then wrap them in a clean dry tea towel and keep the bundle in the middle shelves of your fridge. The same method can be used to keep freshly washed and peeled carrots, topped and tailed green beans, spinach leaves and other fresh vegetables.

Chopped herbs can also be frozen for use in *aashes* and other dishes.

Preparation

Before you wash the herbs, discard any wilting, yellowing or brown leaves. Pick the leaves and discard the stems. In the case of spring onions/scallions, peel off the outer layer and cut off the roots. As a general rule, keep as much of the green part of the stem as the white part and discard the rest.

It is best to wash different herbs separately. Half fill the sink with fresh cold water and drop the herbs in. Move them around gently to loosen any dirt. Gather the leaves from the water and place in a colander. Repeat the process until the water remaining in the sink is clear, then use a salad spinner to

OPPOSITE

A Persian breakfast spread with flat bread.

remove excess water. If you don't have a salad spinner, dry the herbs well in a clean tea towel. The herbs are now ready to eat, or to prepare according to the recipe.

To chop herbs, use a sharp, wide-bladed knife and a chopping board. Food processors are not suitable for this task as they tend to pulp the herbs.

To dry your own herbs, spread them on a large clean cloth after preparing them as above. Leave them to dry slowly over a few days.

Kashk

Kashk is sun-dried whey, left over after butter-making. It is something of an acquired taste. My Western guests almost always remark on its unusual flavour when I use it in a dish; I like to serve it with aubergine/eggplant. It has a higher concentration of protein than any other dairy product: 55 per cent as opposed to around 4 per cent in milk and 20 to 30 per cent in cheese. In Iran, butter is extracted from diluted yogurt, *doogh*. A generous measure of salt is added to the remaining liquid. It is poured into a muslin/cheesecloth bag, drained to a paste, rolled into pieces the size of ping pong balls and left to dry rock hard in the sun. You can buy dried or liquid *kashk* in bottles from Middle Eastern shops.

Storage

It is best to keep *kashk*, whether dried or in liquid form, in the fridge.

Preparation

Dried *kashk* must be mixed with water before use. Follow the instructions on the package; the consistency to aim for is that of double cream.

Lemon and lime juice

Lemon and lime juice lend a subtle tangy flavour to many Persian dishes, from *khoreshts* and *aashes* to salad dressings. You can use fresh lemons or limes, or bottled lemon or lime juice, which can be bought at most supermarkets.

Storage

Store fresh lemons and limes in the fridge for up to three weeks. If buying bottled juice I recommend buying small bottles: it keeps reasonably well in the fridge, but once opened it tends to go bitter after a couple of weeks.

Preparation

Wash and dry the limes or lemons and grate the zest if it is needed in the recipe. Cut them in half and use a lemon juicer to extract the juice. Discard any pips. 1 medium–large lemon yields 3 tablespoons of juice (45–50 ml); 1 lime yields 2 tablespoons of juice (30 ml).

Limes, dried
(*Limoo amaani*)

Typically Persian, dried limes impart a distinctive aroma and piquant flavour; they are essential ingredients in some *khoreshts* and *khoraks*. Dried limes may be used either whole or in powdered form to complement the aromatic herbs or vegetables used in the dish. Adding the dried lime at the beginning of the cooking process will give maximum flavour. Traditionally, however, dried limes are added at a later stage of cooking, so that they are cooked through, but not to the point when they disintegrate. The end result is a very subtle flavour. If you wish, you can add one dried lime per person to the *khoresht* while it is cooking so that everyone can be served with a cooked lime to squeeze with a fork, to add more zest according to personal taste.

Storage

Dried limes, either whole or powdered, can be kept in an airtight jar in a dark cupboard for many months.

Preparation

Wash, dry and pierce the dried lime a couple of times with a fork before adding to the pot. You should push the fork through to the inside of the lime to allow its flavour to seep out and enhance the dish.

Oils and cooking fats

Vegetable oil has now largely replaced the traditional animal fat and clarified butter in Persian cooking. I use sunflower oil, olive oil or lightly salted butter depending on the recipe. I do not generally recommend replacing sunflower oil with olive oil, because the strong and distinctive aroma of the latter may overwhelm the dish. When I use butter for frying I add a little sunflower oil to stop the butter from burning. A small amount of butter is often added to *khoreshts* and rice dishes, either during the cooking or a few minutes before serving, to give the food richness and a subtle flavour.

Storage

Store oils in a dark cupboard.

Pickles
(*Torshi*)

Pickled vegetables and fruit are served as an accompaniment to most Persian meals. Traditionally, each household made its own pickles with seasonal fruit and vegetables. Some, such as garlic pickle, were kept for many years and with the passing of time the interaction between the vegetable and vinegar and spices became more complex. For example, a ten-year-old garlic pickle would taste sweet and the vinegar would be thick and syrupy.

Keep the jar in a dark, cool cupboard. Always make sure the lid
is tightly closed.

Pistachio nuts

Pistachio nuts have very ancient associations with Persia,
and remnants of nuts dating from the sixth millennium BC
have been found in south-eastern Iran. The Persian word for
pistachio, *pesteh*, has given the nut its name in many languages.
Because of its delicate taste and bright green colour, it is used
to decorate dishes such as *Morassa' polo* (p. 155), *Sholleh zard*
(p. 207) and Pistachio ice cream (p. 200). Pistachios are widely
available throughout the world; you can buy them in their
hard shells or already shelled. For use in recipes, be sure to buy
unsalted pistachios.

Storage
Store pistachio nuts in an airtight container in a cool, dark place
for up to a month. In the warmer summer months you should
store them in the fridge.

Preparation
For use in recipes, the nuts should be shelled and the thin skin
removed – by rubbing the nuts in a clean tea towel – to reveal
the bright green kernel. This is then cut into thin slivers.

Pomegranate

Pomegranate, the fruit of a deciduous shrub, *Punica granatum*,
a native plant of Persia, features widely in the country's
cuisine. Pomegranates are thought to have been cultivated
since prehistoric times, and in Iran there are many varieties.
Pomegranate juice, recently celebrated in the West for its
health-giving properties, is commonly sold on Iranian streets.
It is a good source of vitamin C, folic acid/folate and various

antioxidants that are believed to have a wide range of health benefits. Pomegranate seeds are widely used as a garnish for salads such as *Salad-e anar* (p. 173). Pomegranate syrup, also known as pomegranate molasses, pomegranate paste or *Robb-e anar*, is a main ingredient of *Aash-e anar* (p. 41) and *Khoresht-e fesenjan* (p. 70). Jars of concentrated pomegranate syrup are sold in Middle Eastern shops and some supermarkets.

Storage
Store unopened jars and bottles of pomegranate syrup in a cool, dark cupboard. Once opened, store in the fridge for up to four weeks. Store the fresh fruit in a cool place for up to two weeks.

Preparation
Use as directed in the recipe.

To remove the seeds from a fresh pomegranate, use a small sharp knife to cut off the crown. Score through the skin of the pomegranate, dividing it into quarters. Gently pull the pomegranate apart, from the crown downwards, and ease out the juicy red seeds, carefully removing and discarding all the whitish membrane/pith.

Pulses

Pulses (beans, peas and lentils) have been used as food for thousands of years; the lentil was probably one of the first plants to be cultivated. Pulses are an important source of nutrition in Persian food. They are rich in protein, carbohydrate and fibre, and low in fat. They are also good sources of some B vitamins. They can be eaten fresh or dried and come in many varieties, with a range of colours, flavours and textures. The pulses used most frequently in Persian cooking are split peas, chick peas, lentils, red kidney beans and black-eyed beans. The pulses sold in the Middle East have usually been dried in the sun and may require lengthy soaking in cold water before cooking. Varieties available in supermarkets and most shops in the West are dried under factory conditions and often need less soaking (read the instructions on the packet): lentils can be cooked without soaking, while chick peas and red kidney beans will need to be soaked overnight. Canning eliminates the need for soaking and considerably reduces the cooking time compared with dried pulses, but I generally prefer to use dried pulses, except for red kidney beans. In *Khoresht-e ghormeh sabzi* (p. 79) I use canned red kidney beans, which makes the recipe easier and quicker without affecting the taste or the texture. Do not mix dried and canned pulses in the same recipe. A wide variety of dried and canned pulses can be found in supermarkets and specialist stores.

Storage

Keep dried pulses in airtight containers, out of the light, for up to a year.

Preparation

Most dried pulses must be soaked before use; follow the instructions on the packet.

Rice

Rice is integral to Persian cooking: a meal is not considered complete without rice. It serves the same function as potatoes or pasta in the typical Western diet, providing the majority of our daily carbohydrate. I explain the techniques for cooking rice in Chapter 5 (p. 126). When cooking rice as a main dish, with the possible exception of *dampokhtak* (pp. 131, 144), I recommend using basmati rice. The aroma and the texture of this variety are closest to the high-quality rice varieties on sale in Iran, and with basmati rice you are assured of a dish of fluffy long grains of rice separated and perfectly cooked, as long as you follow the recipe. For desserts such as *Sholleh zard* (p. 207) the kind of rice you use is immaterial.

Storage

Store rice in a cool place in an airtight container.

Preparation

I have detailed various ways to cook rice in Chapter 5. You can experiment with the methods to find the one that suits you best.

You can also use a Japanese rice cooker (see Chapter 5) for some recipes.

Rose water and rose petals

Persian cooking makes frequent use of dried rose petals and rose water. Only a few varieties of rose – aromatic with a slightly sweet flavour – are suitable, and harvesting is a delicate process, taking place before sunrise to capture the rose at its best. The petals are spread on sheets to dry under the hot sun. Rose water is extracted from rose petals by distillation: formerly an elaborate and time-consuming process, but nowadays more mechanized and economical. Rose water is mostly used to flavour sweets and desserts such as ice cream and rice pudding. Dried rose petals are crushed and sprinkled over soups such as *Aabdoogh khiar* (p. 51) and side dishes such as *Maast va khiar* (p. 187) as decoration; they are also used in some Persian spice blends (*advieh*).

Sachets of dried rose petals and bottles of rose water are sold in Middle Eastern shops.

Storage

Store unopened sachets of dried rose petals and bottles of rose water in a cool, dark place. Once opened, rose petals don't keep their taste and aroma for long, so transfer the petals to an airtight container and use within two to three weeks. But rose water can be kept in the fridge for a long time, as long as it stays fragrant.

Saffron

Delicate, colourful and intensely aromatic, saffron characterizes Persian cuisine perhaps more than any other spice. Saffron is often added to a dish while it is cooking to enhance the flavour and add depth and complexity to the aroma. A dish of white rice, piled up with light fluffy grains, is usually decorated with a couple of spoonfuls of rice mixed with the yellowy-orange of liquid saffron. A spoonful of this golden liquid, drizzled over the food just before serving, provides a dash of vibrant colour and adds the finishing touch to many *khoreshts* and *aashes*.

The saffron flower is a member of the crocus family; each flower bears three stigmas, which are dried and used for their flavour and colour. Typically, 1 kg/just over 2 lb of spice is extracted from around 500 kg/11,000 lb of harvested flowers. Take care when buying saffron that you are getting the genuine article. The price is one guide: good saffron is expensive. Another sign is the aroma – you should be able to smell the saffron as soon as you open the jar. The colourful part of the strands is said to carry the aroma whereas the threadlike, whitish part has the taste.

Storage

I keep my jar of saffron strands in the freezer. When I have ground the saffron I keep it in the fridge in an airtight container. I usually make enough liquid saffron (see below) to use within a couple of days and keep it in the fridge in a cup covered with foil or cling film.

Preparation

Ground saffron: grind saffron strands with granulated sugar using a pestle and mortar. The hard grains of sugar help grind the strands of saffron to a fine powder. Saffron is usually sold in one-gram boxes or jars. You can grind the entire contents of the package to a fine powder with 1 teaspoon of granulated sugar and keep it in an airtight jar in a cool place or in the fridge. If you are not sure of the quantity, grind ½ teaspoon of saffron strands with approximately ¼ teaspoon of granulated sugar.

Liquid saffron: to extract as much of the aroma and flavour as possible, brew the ground saffron like tea before you use it. Mix ¼ teaspoon of the ground saffron with 4 tablespoons of boiling water in a cup. Stir with a teaspoon, cover the cup and leave to brew for 3–4 minutes before use. Unlike tea, you can keep the liquid saffron for a few days.

Spices

Persian cooking makes extensive use of spices. The most widely utilized ones are: black pepper, green cardamom, cinnamon, coriander seeds, cumin, *golpar* (p. 17), nutmeg, rose petals (p.26), saffron (p. 27) and turmeric (p. 30).

Advieh is the term for various blends of spices that are used to season *khoreshts*, *khoraks* and rice dishes. The blends vary from region to region but usually include cinnamon, cumin, nutmeg and sometimes ground coriander seeds. *Advieh* is sold in sachets in Middle Eastern and Iranian shops.

Fresh or dried chillies, small but very hot, green or red, are frequently used in Persian dishes.

Storage

Keep spices in airtight containers in a cool, dark place for two to three months.

Sumac

Sumac is a spice made from the red berries that appear in dense clusters on bushes of a plant that grows wild throughout Iran. The berries are dried and crushed to form a coarse purple-red powder. Sumac has a distinct and slightly aromatic sour taste. In Iran, sumac is used as a condiment, sprinkled on *Chelo kabab*

(p. 103), a dish of plain rice and barbecued meat. Packets of sumac powder are sold in Middle Eastern shops.

Once opened, keep the sumac powder in an airtight container in a cool, dark place for four to six months.

Tamarind

The fruit of the tamarind tree is covered in a long, hard shell that turns brown when ripe; inside the shell the seeds are surrounded by fleshy pulp. In Persian cooking, tamarind is used to give dishes an intriguing sweet and sour flavour. Its use in Persian recipes reflects the influence of Indian cuisine, and tamarind mostly appears in dishes from southern Iran, such as Okra and lamb *khoresht* (p. 68) and *Ghalyeh mahi* (p. 75), a fish *khoresht*.

You can buy tamarind in various forms, but the best type to use for Persian cooking is a concentrated tamarind paste. Two kinds are quite widely available in specialist shops and larger supermarkets: the Indian version is more tangy and the Thai one is sweeter; you can use either.

Storage

Keep the unopened jar or packet in a cupboard; once opened, transfer to the fridge and keep to the 'use by' date on the packaging.

Preparation

Put the tamarind paste into a small bowl and add boiling water, as directed in the recipe. Leave to stand for 10–15 minutes. Stir well to dissolve the paste in the water. Pass the liquid through a fine sieve to separate any stringy bits or stones that might have been left in the paste.

Tomato purée/tomato paste

Widely used in Persian cooking, in rice dishes, *khoreshts*, *khoraks* and other dishes. Traditionally, in Iran, tomatoes are partially dried in the heat of the sun before the skins and seeds are separated from the pulp. The pulp is then spread on trays and set under the sun to lose its water content. Nowadays tomato purée is readily available in cans, tubes or bottles. The nearest in taste to the Persian version is that made from sundried tomatoes, which is sold in many supermarkets and delicatessens.

Storage

Store at room temperature before opening; once opened, store in the fridge.

Preparation

Dilute with water if required by the recipe.

Turmeric

Turmeric is derived from the rhizomes (rootlike stems) of *Curcuma longa*, a plant native to southern Asia. Turmeric has rough brown skin and deep orange flesh, but is usually dried and ground for use as a spice. In Chinese and Indian traditional medicine it is considered a potent anti-inflammatory. In Persian cookery, turmeric is used in the preparation of almost all *aashes* and *khoreshts*. It lends its deep yellow colour to the food and accentuates flavours that would otherwise remain bland. It gives a distinctive taste to fried onions, which in turn enhance the aroma and flavour of the dish they are incorporated in. It also helps reduce the sometimes powerful aroma of lamb. Ground turmeric is readily available from supermarkets and Middle Eastern or Indian shops.

Storage

Store in an airtight jar in a cool, dark cupboard for up to six months.

Walnuts

Walnuts are the edible seeds of an ornamental tree that
is also highly prized for its timber. The nut kernels of all
walnut species are edible, but the walnuts most commonly
available in shops are from the Persian walnut (also known
as English walnut and, in the UK, common walnut). They are
an excellent source of protein and omega-3 fatty acids, are
rich in fibre, vitamins and minerals, and have been shown to
lower cholesterol and help prevent heart disease. Walnuts are
a traditional feature of Persian cuisine, cooked in main dishes
like *Khoresht-e fesenjan* (p. 70) where the nutty flavour combines
with the sweet and sour taste of pomegranate syrup. They are
also added to cold yogurt-based side dishes such as *Borani-e
esfenaj* (p. 182) and *Maast va karafs* (p. 184).

Walnuts are sold ready shelled in most supermarkets. In Iran
we try to buy from the current year's harvest, but I imagine it
would be almost impossible to establish how old the nuts are
when buying them in the West.

Storage

As they are high in fat, walnuts need to be kept cool and dry; in
warm conditions the fat will become rancid in a few weeks.

Preparation

If you have bought walnuts in their hard shells, you will need to
crack and remove the shells before weighing them to use in the
recipe. If a recipe calls for walnuts to be chopped, I generally
prefer to do this by hand; if you use a food processor, take care
not to overgrind them or they will lose their oil. However,
when a larger quantity of walnuts is needed, for example for
Khoresht-e fesenjan (p. 70), it is easier to use a food processor.

Yogurt

Yogurt is the result of fermentation of milk, a way of concentrating and preserving the goodness of milk for longer. In this book I recommend Greek-style full-fat/whole milk yogurt, which is the closest I have found to *Maast-e kisseh*, a thickened yogurt used in Iran. No Persian spread would be complete without at least one side dish made with yogurt. Wholesome, refreshing and inexpensive, yogurt is a good source of protein and vitamins; it aids digestion and is eaten to clean the palate in between helpings of rich and complex dishes.

Storage

Store in the fridge and eat fresh, within the 'use by' date.

Preparation

To make authentic *Maast-e kisseh*, take a muslin/cheesecloth bag, pour a tub of full-fat yogurt into it and hang it over a bowl for up to 24 hours. The excess water gradually drains out and you are left with a paste-like yogurt, about a half to a third of the original volume.

Verjuice

Verjuice is the juice of unripe grapes, which are picked in early summer to encourage the grapes left on the vine to grow bigger. It gives a delicate tart flavour to dishes such as Aubergine and lamb *khoresht* (*Khoresht-e badenjan*, p. 65). Verjuice is bottled for use throughout the year and is available from Middle Eastern stores.

Storage

Buy in small bottles and store in a dark cupboard. Once opened, store in the fridge for up to three weeks.

OPPOSITE

Door showing a carving of a soldier from the Achaemenid era, when the Persian Empire was at its height.

Chapter 2

Aashes and other soups

*A*ashes are rich, hearty soups with a very thick consistency. They are a particular feature of Persian cooking and are enjoyed all over the country, each region having its own favourites. Recipes vary according to the area and the seasonal availability of herbs (dried herbs may be used in winter).

Aashes are filling and nutritious and are often eaten as a main meal with bread. When serving as a main course, you can add Miniature meatballs (*Koofteh ghelgheli*, p. 108) to some *aashes* before serving (as indicated in the recipe).

OPPOSITE

Aash-e anar is a delicately balanced sweet and sour soup with herbs and pomegranate syrup (see p. 41).

The secret to a good *aash* is to get the base mixture right. For most *aashes* this consists of onions, split peas or other pulses, rice and a variety of fresh herbs. The onions should be fried until golden to lend aroma and flavour to the finished soup; the pulses and rice are cooked until they are completely soft and broken down so that they thicken the soup.

Use a heavy-based pan for even distribution of heat and stir the *aash* frequently all the way through the cooking process to make sure that it does not stick to the bottom of the pan.

Shoorba, a version of *aash*, is made with chicken or vegetable stock and rice (but no pulses) as the base ingredients, combined with spinach, coriander/cilantro and sometimes parsley. It is a light and simple soup usually served to boost strength after an illness.

Thin soups, closer to Western soups, are more recent additions to Persian cuisine. The exception, *eshkeneh* (p. 52) – an onion and fenugreek soup mixed with egg – is a very old recipe that is said to date back to the Sassanian period (AD 224–651). Once considered a peasant dish, *eshkeneh* has recently been rediscovered as a very tasty first course.

Almost all *aashes* and soups make delicious vegetarian dishes if vegetable stock is used; chicken stock gives a richer flavour.

As a general rule, *aashes* can be prepared a day in advance, kept in the fridge and reheated before serving.

Almost invariably the *aash* will become thick and set as it cools; when reheating you will need to stir in enough boiling water to return it to its original consistency.

※

Lamb soup with pulses
Abgusht

This is a rich and nutritious dish, suitable for cold winter days. It combines complex carbohydrates, protein and fat, and with side dishes of fresh herbs and yogurt it makes a healthy balanced meal. Traditionally a poor man's dish, it has come into its own in recent years for informal family meals. It used to be made with the cheapest cuts of lamb and animal fat. In the old tea houses and caravanserai, specially made individual clay pots were used to make *abgusht*. All the ingredients were put into the pot, a small quantity of water added and the lid was then sealed with mud. The pots were buried in the ashes of the wood stove and left to cook slowly. Today, better-quality cuts of lamb such as leg or shoulder shanks are used. Traditionally, the broth is strained off and served as a soup with pieces of bread floating on the surface like croutons. The meat and pulses are pounded together and eaten with fresh herbs and warm flat bread.

The ingredients of *abgusht* vary from region to region. The most common version uses only chick peas and no tomato purée/ tomato paste. The recipe given here includes potatoes, red kidney beans and split peas, as well as tomato purée. It is a very easy dish to make, but it has to be cooked slowly in order for the flavours to develop. You can make it a day in advance to the stage of adding the red kidney beans; to serve, reheat it, then add the lemon juice and saffron just before serving.

Preparation
Wash the split peas, put them in a bowl, pour boiling water over them and soak for 1 hour (or follow the instructions on the packet). Alternatively, soak the split peas in cold water overnight.

Serves 4–6
Preparation: approximately 30 minutes, plus soaking
Cooking: approximately 2½ hours

Ingredients
100 g/3½ oz split peas
4 lamb shoulder shanks (or 3 leg shanks)
1 large onion
3 medium potatoes
2 tablespoons vegetable oil
2 teaspoons turmeric
2 dried limes, washed, dried and pierced with a fork (p. 21)
1 litre/1¾ pints boiling water
2 heaped teaspoons tomato purée/tomato paste
salt and black pepper
200 g/7 oz canned red kidney beans (drained weight)
3 tablespoons lemon juice
2 tablespoons liquid saffron (p. 28)

The traditional way to serve
abgusht is to strain the liquid
into bowls to serve as a broth,
then pound the cooked
meat and other ingredients
in a food processor or
using a pestle and mortar
or potato masher. You can
pound the mixture until it
is smooth or for a shorter
period to retain the texture
of the components. This
is called *Gusht-e koubideh*:
literally, pounded meat.
Serve separately on a platter
with peeled, quartered fresh
onions and warm flat bread.
The meat can also be eaten
cold as a sandwich filling in
pitta bread.

Wash the lamb shanks and pat them dry with kitchen paper.
Cut off any skin, protruding tendon and fat with a sharp knife.

Peel the onion and cut it into quarters. Peel the potatoes and
cut each one into four. Place the potato pieces in a bowl and
cover with cold water to avoid discoloration.

Cooking
Heat the oil in a heavy-based saucepan, preferably cast-iron,
and toss the quartered onion in the oil for a couple of minutes,
until lightly golden. Add the lamb shanks and turn to seal on all
sides. The meat should not be browned at this stage.

Add the turmeric and stir to coat the shanks evenly. Drain the
split peas and add to the pan, then add the dried limes.

Pour the boiling water into the pan and stir well. Bring back
to the boil, then reduce the heat and cover the pan with a lid.
Simmer gently for approximately 1½ hours until the shanks are
nearly cooked (you should be able to separate the meat from the
bone with a fork) and the split peas are al dente. Keep the heat
low and keep the lid on the pan to retain as much of the liquid
as possible.

Drain and add the potatoes and the tomato purée/tomato paste
to the pan and stir to mix. Leave to simmer very gently until the
potatoes are cooked, approximately 30 minutes. Season to taste.

Add the red kidney beans and simmer for a further
10–15 minutes. Add the lemon juice and simmer for another 5
minutes. Just before serving, add the liquid saffron and mix well.

Serve with warm flat bread such as pitta or *lavash* (very thin
Persian bread) with a side dish of yogurt and fresh herbs (*sabzi
khordan*, p. 17).

Herb and pomegranate soup
Aash-e anar

This is a hearty winter dish that can be served as a vegetarian main course or first course. Its subtle sweet and sour taste comes from the pomegranate syrup. There are many versions of *aash-e anar*; my recipe uses generous quantities of fresh herbs to give a wonderfully aromatic result. Although this recipe takes time to prepare, the result is worth it – and you can cook the *aash* from start to finish in one saucepan.

Preparation
Wash the split peas in several changes of cold water. It is best to soak the peas before using: follow the instructions on the packet, or in the absence of instructions allow at least 2 hours.

Wash the rice in several changes of cold water until the water remains reasonably clear. Drain the rice, tip into a bowl and add enough cold water to cover the rice. Add 1 teaspoon of salt. Leave to soak for 2 hours.

Spread out the herbs and pinch off the leaves and tender stalks, discarding the tougher stalks and any wilting and yellowing leaves. Wash the herbs in plenty of cold water, then use a salad spinner or shake well to get rid of excess water. Chop the herbs finely with a sharp, wide-bladed knife. (The mountain of leaves you started off with should be reduced to a small mound.) You can chop the herbs while the split peas and rice are cooking or prepare them up to 24 hours in advance: place in a bowl, cover with a damp cloth and keep in the fridge.

Peel and finely chop the onion.

Serves 4–6
Preparation: approximately
1 hour, plus soaking
Cooking: approximately
2½ hours

Ingredients
150 g/5 oz yellow split peas
100 g/3½ oz rice (any variety)
salt and black pepper
450 g/1 lb fresh herbs:
150 g/5 oz coriander/cilantro,
200 g/7 oz flat-leafed parsley and
100 g/3½ oz dill (or 20 g/¾ oz
dried dill if fresh is not available)
1 medium onion
50 g/2 oz butter
2 tablespoons sunflower oil
2 litres/3½ pints boiling water
2 tablespoons turmeric
2 stock cubes, chicken (or
vegetable)
300 ml/10 fl oz pomegranate
syrup (p. 24)
2 tablespoons sugar

Garnish
30 g/1 oz butter
4 tablespoons sunflower oil
2 tablespoons dried mint
30 g/1 oz walnuts, chopped

See p. 37 for recipe image.

Cooking

Heat the butter and oil together in a large, heavy-based saucepan on a medium to high heat. Add the onion and fry until soft and golden.

Drain the split peas and add to the pan, stir a couple of times. Add about 1 litre/1¾ pints of the boiling water and bring back to the boil. Cover the pan with a lid and reduce the heat. Do not add salt at this stage. Leave to simmer until the split peas are completely cooked (approximately 1 hour). They should be soft enough to squash easily between your thumb and forefinger.

Drain the rice and add to the pan. Add the rest of the boiling water and simmer for 30 minutes, until the rice is almost dissolved (you should not be able to see the separate grains any more), stirring occasionally to prevent the mixture from sticking to the bottom of the pan. You can add more boiling water to the pan at any stage to adjust the consistency of the *aash*.

Add the herbs, the turmeric and the stock cubes. Simmer gently for another 30 minutes, stirring frequently.

Stir in the pomegranate syrup and sugar, and simmer on a very low heat for a further 20 minutes. The result will be a thick, dark green soup, with a rich aroma of herbs and a subtle sweet and sour taste. Taste and adjust the seasoning.

Garnish

In a small pan, heat the butter with 3 tablespoons of oil. When hot, add the dried mint and remove from the heat immediately. Heat the remaining oil in a separate small pan, add the chopped walnuts, stir and remove from the heat immediately.

Serve the *aash* in a large bowl, and drizzle the garnish over it. For a main course, serve with fresh bread.

VARIATION

If the *aash* is a main course, you can add Miniature meatballs (p. 108) to the pan about 10 minutes before serving.

Barley and herb soup
Aash-e jo

This hearty *aash* is an ideal winter dish. Serve with fresh bread and a side salad for a satisfying vegetarian lunch.

Preparation
Wash the barley in cold water. Drain, then put the barley in a bowl, cover with cold water and soak for 2 hours. Do the same with the rice.

Wash the parsley and use a salad spinner to get rid of the excess water. Pinch off the leaves and discard the stalks. Chop the parsley finely with a sharp, wide-bladed knife. Set aside.

Rinse the chives, keeping them in a bundle. Cut them into small pieces, 2–3 mm/about 1/8 inch in length, and add them to the parsley. If you are using spring onions/scallions, wash them, then cut off the roots and discard. Cut the spring onions lengthwise twice before bundling them up and cutting them as directed for the chives.

Peel the onion, cut it into four or six pieces and set aside.

Heat half of the sunflower oil in a small pan. Add the dried mint and stir a couple of times to mix. Remove from the heat and set aside.

Cooking
Heat the remaining 3 tablespoons of sunflower oil in a large, heavy-based saucepan. Add the onion and fry until golden.

Drain the barley and add to the pan. Stir to coat the grains of barley in oil and add 1 litre/1¾ pints of boiling water. Bring

Serves 4–6
Preparation: approximately 45 minutes, plus soaking
Cooking: approximately 2 hours

Ingredients
150 g/5 oz pearl barley
50 g/2 oz rice (any variety)
200 g/7 oz flat-leafed parsley (or 4 tablespoons dried parsley)
100 g/3½ oz chives (or the green parts of fresh young spring onions/scallions)
1 medium onion
6 tablespoons sunflower oil
2 tablespoons dried mint
2 litres/3½ pints boiling water
500 ml/approximately 1 pint chicken/vegetable stock (or 1 stock cube dissolved in 500 ml boiling water)
2 teaspoons turmeric
3–4 tablespoons lemon juice (use less if you want a less tangy taste)
salt and black pepper

Garnish
4 tablespoons sunflower oil
1 small onion, peeled and thinly sliced
2 tablespoons dried mint

VARIATIONS
Some versions of *Aash-e jo* include chunks of shoulder of lamb, cooked separately and added to the *aash* to simmer for 5 minutes before serving. You need 500 g/1 lb 2 oz shoulder of lamb (including the bone). Lightly fry the meat in 2 tablespoons of vegetable oil with 1 chopped small onion, add 1 litre/1¾ pints of boiling water and simmer on a low heat for about 2 hours until the meat is cooked and can be easily separated from the bone.

Miniature meatballs (p. 108) also go well with this *aash*; add them 10 minutes before serving.

back to the boil and reduce the heat, stirring occasionally. Simmer gently until the barley is very tender (approximately 40 minutes). You should be able to squash the grains between your thumb and forefinger.

Drain the rice and add to the pan with 500ml/approximately 1 pint of boiling water. Simmer until the rice is very tender (approximately 30 minutes), stirring occasionally to prevent the rice from sticking to the bottom of the pan. If necessary, add more hot water to maintain a thick soup-like consistency.

Add the stock, chopped herbs and turmeric to the pan. Stir thoroughly and simmer for another 15 minutes to cook the herbs.

Add the lemon juice, and salt and pepper to taste and simmer for a further 5 minutes. Add the prepared mint in oil and stir well.

Garnish
Heat the oil in a small frying pan/skillet and fry the sliced onion until crisp and golden brown. Add the dried mint, stir a couple of times and remove from the heat.

Serve the *aash* in a shallow bowl and garnish with the fried onion and mint.

❋

Dill, mint and yogurt soup
Aash-e maast

The combination of dill, mint and yogurt is a very particular fresh taste, and this *aash* can be made all year round, replacing fresh dill with dried in winter (it is one of the few recipes that taste equally nice with either). You can also make this *aash* thinner and serve it as a first course. It is very popular at parties!

Preparation
Wash the split peas in cold water, drain, then soak in cold water for at least 2 hours (or follow the instructions on the packet).

Wash the rice in several changes of cold water until the water remains reasonably clear. Drain, then soak in cold water for 2 hours.

If using fresh dill, wash it in cold water and use a salad spinner or shake well to remove as much of the water as possible. Pinch off the leaves and tender stalks and discard the thicker, tougher stalks. Pile up the leaves on a chopping board and chop them finely with a sharp, wide-bladed knife.

Peel and finely chop the onion.

Cooking
Melt the butter in a large, heavy-based saucepan, add the oil, then fry the chopped onion until soft and golden.

Drain the split peas and add to the onion, stirring a couple of times to coat the peas in oil. Add about half of the stock and bring back to the boil. Do not add salt at this stage. Cover the pan with a lid and reduce the heat. Leave to simmer until the split peas are completely cooked (approximately 1 hour). They

Serves 4–6
Preparation: 20–30 minutes, plus soaking
Cooking: 2–2½ hours

Ingredients
150 g/5 oz split peas
100 g/3½ oz rice (any variety)
100 g/3½ oz fresh dill (or 4 tablespoons dried dill)
1 medium onion
30 g/1 oz butter
4 tablespoons vegetable oil
2 litres/3½ pints chicken/vegetable stock (or 4 stock cubes dissolved in 2 litres boiling water)
2 teaspoons turmeric
4 tablespoons lemon juice
450 g/1 lb Greek-style full-fat/whole milk yogurt
salt and black pepper

Garnish
4 tablespoons sunflower oil
1 medium onion, peeled and thinly sliced
3 cloves of garlic, finely chopped
20 g/¾ oz butter
3 tablespoons dried mint

should be soft enough to squash between your thumb and forefinger.

Drain the rice and add to the pan. Add the rest of the stock and simmer for a further 30 minutes, until the rice is completely cooked (on the point of disintegration), stirring occasionally to stop the mixture from sticking to the bottom of the pan.

Add the finely chopped fresh dill (or dried dill) and turmeric to the pan. If necessary, add small amounts of boiling water to produce a smooth but thick consistency (add more water if you want the soup to be a bit thinner).

Let the soup simmer for a further 30 minutes on a low heat, stirring occasionally. Remove from the heat and leave to stand for 5 minutes.

Mix the lemon juice with the yogurt and add to the pan, stirring all the while to mix thoroughly. Taste and adjust the seasoning.

Just before serving, reheat the *aash* on a low heat for a few minutes, taking care that it does not come to the boil. If it boils the yogurt will separate, affecting the appearance of the dish.

Garnish

Heat 3 tablespoons of the oil in a small frying pan/skillet. Add the sliced onion and fry until light brown. Add the chopped garlic, stir and set aside. Heat the butter with the rest of the oil in another small pan. Add the dried mint, stir and remove from the heat immediately.

Serve the *aash* in a shallow bowl and garnish with the fried onion and mint.

OPPOSITE

Aash-e maast is a thick and hearty soup flavoured with creamy yogurt.

Serves 6–8
Preparation: approximately
1 hour, plus soaking
Cooking: approximately 2½ hours

Ingredients
50 g/2 oz mung beans
50 g/2 oz split peas
50 g/2 oz green lentils
50 g/2 oz red kidney beans
50 g/2 oz black-eyed beans (or
white beans such as cannellini)
50 g/2 oz chick peas
50 g/2 oz rice (any variety)
salt and black pepper
1 large onion
150 g/5 oz spinach or (beetroot/
beet leaves)
100 g/3½ oz fresh dill
100 g/3½ oz fresh coriander/
cilantro
100 g/3½ oz fresh parsley
100 g/3½ oz fresh chives (or
green parts of spring onions/
scallions)
50 g/2 oz fresh tarragon (or 2
tablespoons dried)
30 g/1 oz fresh *marzeh* (summer
savory) (optional)
50 g/2 oz butter
4 tablespoons sunflower oil
2 litres/3½ pints boiling water
3 chicken/vegetable
stock cubes
1 teaspoon turmeric

Mixed pulses and herb soup
Aash-e sholleh ghalamkar

One of the most delicious and nutritious *aashes*; serve with hot bread for a substantial meal. *Aash-e sholleh ghalamkar* goes very well with yogurt as a side dish. In Iran it is often served with *kashk* (p. 20). *Kashk* is sold in liquid or powdered form in Middle Eastern stores.

My recipe uses chicken (or vegetable) stock, which allows the flavour of the herbs to shine through. In Iran the soup is made from cuts of rib, shoulder or neck of lamb, giving it a viscous consistency and a more meaty flavour.

The types of herbs – and their proportions – vary between different recipes. This version favours the aromatic dominance of tarragon, and also includes spinach or beetroot/beet leaves. Most traditional recipes use *marzeh* (summer savory), a popular herb in Iran. It is not essential, but if you can find the fresh herb it adds to the aroma.

Aash-e sholleh ghalamkar takes time to prepare and cook, but the result is well worth it. You can make this *aash* a couple of days in advance, keep it in the fridge and reheat it gently before serving.

Preparation
Wash all the pulses in cold water, then soak them in cold water overnight.

Wash the rice in several changes of cold water until the water remains reasonably clear. Drain the rice, tip into a bowl and add enough cold water to cover the rice. Add 1 teaspoon of salt. Leave to soak for 2 hours.

Peel and chop the onion.

Spread out the herbs and pinch off the leaves and tender stalks
to separate them from the tougher stalks, discarding wilting
and yellowing leaves. Wash them in plenty of cold water and
use a salad spinner or shake well to get rid of excess water.
Chop the herbs finely with a sharp, wide-bladed knife, reducing
the mountain of leaves you started off with to a small mound.
Set aside. If you chop the herbs in advance, keep them fresh by
covering with a damp tea towel in the fridge.

Cooking

Use a large, heavy-based saucepan (pulses expand considerably
when cooked, so be sure your pan is big enough). Put the pan
on a medium to high heat, add the butter, then add the oil and
fry the chopped onion until soft and golden.

Drain the pulses and add them to the pan. Stir to coat the pulses
thoroughly in oil. Add 1 litre/1¾ pints of the boiling water and
bring back to the boil. Do not add salt at this stage. Cover the
pan with a lid and reduce the heat. Simmer for approximately
1½ hours until all the pulses are very tender. You should be
able to squash any of the beans or peas between your thumb
and forefinger.

Drain the rice and add to the pan. Crumble the stock cubes
and add to the pan with the rest of the water. Simmer for
30 minutes until the rice is completely cooked (you should
not be able to see whole grains of rice), stirring occasionally to
prevent the mixture from sticking to the bottom of the pan.

Add the herbs and the turmeric. Taste and adjust the seasoning.
Simmer gently on a low heat for a further 30 minutes, stirring
frequently. It is important to cook this *aash* slowly so that the
herbs' aroma can develop and diffuse into the mixture.

Garnish

4 tablespoons sunflower oil
1 medium onion, peeled and
thinly sliced
2 large cloves of garlic, finely
chopped
20 g/¾ oz butter
1 tablespoon dried mint

Garnish

Heat 3 tablespoons of the oil in a small frying pan/skillet, add the sliced onion and fry until light brown. Add the chopped garlic, stir and set aside. Heat the butter with the remaining oil in a separate small pan. Add the dried mint, stir and remove from the heat immediately.

Pour the *aash* into a large soup bowl and garnish with the fried onion and mint.

Right: One of the many breathtaking waterfalls in central Iran.

Chilled cucumber soup with yogurt and herbs
Aabdoogh khiar

Serves 4-6
Preparation: 10–15 minutes, plus chilling

This cold, yogurt-based soup is fantastic as a first course on hot summer days. It can be as thin or as rich as you like: experiment to establish your favourite consistency. Dried mint is essential and preferable to fresh mint in this dish because it gives a more intense flavour; fresh herbs add texture, aroma and flavour, while raisins and nuts complete the palette.

Ingredients
250 g/9 oz cucumber (preferably the small Middle Eastern variety, p. 14)
100 g/3½ oz raisins (or sultanas/ golden raisins)
50 g/2 oz walnuts, finely chopped
250 g/9 oz Greek-style full-fat/ whole milk yogurt
1 litre/1¾ pints cold water
20 g/¾ oz fresh herbs: tarragon, basil or parsley (optional)
2 teaspoons dried mint
salt and black pepper

Preparation
Grate the cucumber into a large bowl. Add the raisins or sultanas, walnuts and yogurt. Add the cold water and mix thoroughly, whisking the mixture with a fork.

If using fresh herbs, wash and dry them, then chop finely, using a sharp, wide-bladed knife. Add the dried mint and the fresh herbs to the yogurt mixture. Season with salt and pepper to taste and stir. Chill in the fridge for at least 1 hour (you can make this a day in advance and keep it chilled) and stir well before serving.

This is a thirst-quenching and refreshing summer soup and is meant to have a light herby taste.

Serves 4–6
Preparation: approximately
30 minutes
Cooking: approximately 1 hour

Ingredients

1 medium onion

250 g/9 oz potatoes

50 g/2 oz celery

30 g/1 oz fresh coriander/
cilantro

30 g/1 oz butter

2 tablespoons sunflower oil

4 tablespoons dried fenugreek

1 teaspoon turmeric

1 litre/1¾ pints chicken or
vegetable stock (or 2 stock cubes
dissolved in 1 litre boiling water)

1 egg, beaten

juice of ½ lemon

salt and black pepper

Garnish (optional)

20 g/¾ oz butter

2 tablespoons sunflower oil

1 medium onion, peeled and
thinly sliced

Fenugreek soup
Eshkeneh

This light soup has a delicate but distinct fenugreek flavour. Quick and easy to make, it can be served as a first course or as a light lunch with a couple of chunky slices of warm wholemeal bread or flat bread. This recipe dates back to the Sassanian period (224–651 AD) and after a period of neglect, it has become fashionable once again.

There are many versions of *Eshkeneh*, ranging from simple recipes like this one to more elaborate soups made with quince, sour cherries or pomegranate syrup. This is my favourite adaptation; it uses celery and coriander/cilantro as well as fenugreek.

Preparation

Peel and finely chop the onion. Peel the potatoes and cut into small dice, about ½ cm/¼ inch across. Wash the celery sticks and cut lengthwise into strips. Bundle them together and cut into 2–3mm/ 1/8 inch pieces.

Wash the coriander/cilantro and dry in a salad spinner or shake well to remove excess water. Pinch off the leaves and tender stalks, discarding the tougher stalks. Chop the coriander finely, using a sharp, wide-bladed knife.

Cooking

Heat the butter and oil together in a medium-sized, heavy based saucepan on a medium to high heat. Add the chopped onion and fry until soft and golden.

Add the potato, celery, coriander, fenugreek and turmeric to the fried onions. Stir well and fry for a further 3–5 minutes on a medium heat. Add the stock, stir well and simmer for 30-40 minutes on a very low heat.

When all the ingredients are cooked and soft, blend briefly: there should still be recognizable pieces of vegetable in the mixture.

Return the blended soup to the pan on a low heat. Whisk in the beaten egg. Add the lemon juice and salt and pepper to taste. Let the soup simmer for a further 5 minutes.

Garnish
Heat the butter and the oil together in a small frying pan/skillet and fry the sliced onion until crisp and light brown.

Serve in a large soup bowl and garnish with fried onions, if using.

Serves 4–6
Preparation: 20-25 minutes
Cooking: approximately 1 hour

Ingredients

1 poussin (or 2 wings and
2 drumsticks of chicken)

1 medium onion

200 g/7 oz potatoes

50 g/2 oz celery

50 g/2 oz fresh coriander/
cilantro

30 g/1 oz butter

2 tablespoons olive oil

1 vegetable stock cube

500 ml/approximately 1 pint
water

salt and black pepper

juice of 1 lemon (use more if you
prefer a tangier flavour)

Chicken and fresh coriander soup
Soup-e joojeh

Chicken soup with a Persian twist.

Preparation
Wash, skin and dry the poussin or chicken pieces.

Peel and finely chop the onion. Peel the potatoes and cut into small dice, about ½ cm/¼ inch across. Wash the celery sticks and cut lengthwise into strips. Bundle them together and cut into 2–3mm/ 1/8 inch pieces. Wash the coriander/cilantro and dry in a salad spinner. Chop the coriander finely, using a sharp, wide-bladed knife.

Cooking
Heat the butter and oil together in a medium-sized, heavy-based saucepan. Add the chopped onion and fry until soft and golden. Add the poussin or chicken pieces, stir well, and fry for a couple of minutes.

Add the potato, celery and half of the coriander with the crumbled stock cube. Reduce the heat, cover and cook very gently for 4–5 minutes.

Add the water and bring to the boil. Reduce the heat to low and simmer gently for 40–45 minutes. Remove the poussin or chicken pieces with a slotted spoon. Take the meat off the bones, using a knife and fork, and cut into pieces; set aside. Blend the rest of the soup until smooth. Return the chicken pieces to the pan and simmer for 10 minutes.

Just before serving add the lemon juice and the rest of the coriander/cilantro.

Winter vegetable soup
Soup-e makhloot

This is a delicious winter soup, although you can make it with seasonal vegetables at any time of the year.

Preparation
Peel the onion and chop it into small pieces. Peel the potatoes and cut into 2 cm/$\frac{3}{4}$ inch cubes. Peel the carrots and slice thinly. Wash and trim the leeks and celery, and cut them into 1 cm/$\frac{1}{2}$ inch thick slices. Wash the baby turnips.

Wash and dry the chives for the garnish. Bundle them up and cut them into 5 mm/$\frac{1}{4}$ inch lengths. Set aside. Wash the parsley and coriander/cilantro and dry in a salad spinner. Roughly chop the herbs with a sharp, wide-bladed knife; set aside.

Cooking
Heat the butter and oil together in a large, heavy-based saucepan. Add the onion and fry until lightly golden. Add the chopped vegetables and herbs and stir to mix them thoroughly. Reduce the heat and let the mixture cook gently for 5–10 minutes. Add the baby turnips and stir again. Pour in the stock and simmer for 45 minutes to 1 hour on a very low heat.

When the vegetables are soft, remove the pan from the heat. Lift out the baby turnips using a slotted spoon and set aside. Blend the rest of the soup briefly. Return the turnips to the saucepan. Add the lemon juice and salt and pepper to taste. Cook for another 10–15 minutes on a low heat, stirring occasionally.

Pour into a serving bowl and garnish with the chopped chives, adding cream if you like.

Serves 4–6
Preparation: approximately 30 minutes
Cooking: approximately 1 $\frac{1}{4}$ hours

Ingredients
1 medium onion
150 g/5 oz potatoes
100 g/3$\frac{1}{2}$ oz carrots
100 g/3$\frac{1}{2}$ oz leeks
100 g/3$\frac{1}{2}$ oz celery
100 g/3$\frac{1}{2}$ oz baby turnips
30 g/1 oz fresh parsley
30 g/1 oz fresh coriander/cilantro
50 g/2 oz butter
4 tablespoons vegetable oil
1 litre/1$\frac{3}{4}$ pints chicken/vegetable stock (or 2 stock cubes dissolved in 1 litre boiling water)
3–4 tablespoons lemon juice
salt and black pepper

Garnish
20 g/$\frac{3}{4}$ oz chives
2 tablespoons single cream/light cream (optional)

Chapter 3

KHORESHTS

Chapter 3

Khoreshts

*K*horeshts are an essential element of Persian cuisine. The nearest equivalent in the West would be a casserole, a rich dish with plenty of sauce. *Khoreshts* may be made from meat, chicken or fish combined with vegetables, herbs, fruits or pulses.

A *khoresht* is almost always served with plain rice (*chelo*); neither dish is secondary or subservient to the other. Serve a couple of large spoonfuls of rice with one large spoonful of *khoresht*; eat the rice and *khoresht* together.

The ingredients in a *khoresht* reflect the changing seasons, drawing on the freshest produce to bring vitamins, minerals and protein into everyday meals. There are numerous varieties of *khoresht*, and each region of Iran puts its own stamp on the dish. Some, such as *Ghormeh sabzi* (p. 79) or *Gheimeh* (p. 77) are popular throughout the country, although there are regional variations.

Khoreshts in the north of Iran tend to have more sauce and are more sweet and sour in flavour; those from the south are spicier, with a distinct piquant taste, and are allowed to simmer longer, resulting in less sauce. The recipes in this book, reflecting my southern origins, adopt the latter style.

Some general rules apply to the cooking of *khoreshts*. The meat, traditionally lamb, is almost always cooked in the same way

OPPOSITE

Top: Khoresht-e seebzamini. *Traditionally khoreshts are served with white rice; here we have plain rice decorated with saffron served with a helping of lamb and potato khoresht (see p. 85).*

Bottom: Khoresht-e fesenjan *(see p. 70).*

initially, before introducing other ingredients. Leg of lamb is the usual cut for *khoreshts* (in Iran the leg bone is included in the *khoresht* for flavour), but shoulder of lamb – which is preferred for roasting – can also be used. You can replace lamb with beef, but the texture and taste of the *khoresht* will not be the same; lamb's distinctive aroma and tenderness is replaced with deeper notes of flavour and tougher texture. Avoid using meat that has been frozen: fresh lamb cooks and tastes better, while frozen meat in general is less flavoursome.

A *khoresht* for 4–6 people will usually include one or two chopped onions, fried in oil until golden brown. Meat is then added to the pan and cooked to seal, until it just begins to change colour. Liquid is added and the *khoresht* is left to simmer gently so that all the ingredients marry together and develop maximum flavour.

Most *khoreshts* can also be made without meat. They make wonderful vegetarian dishes as the other ingredients give depth of flavour and good nutritional balance.

✳

Sweet and sour *khoresht* with spinach and prunes

Khoresht-e aloo esfenaj

Serves 4–6
Preparation: 30 minutes
Cooking: approximately
1 ¾ hours

The combination of spinach and prunes works well and the lemon juice sharpens the sweetness with a delicate, piquant edge. In this recipe, sugar creates a sweet and sour taste, and tomato purée/tomato paste intensifies the colour. Some versions of the dish do not add sugar and the final taste is quite tart, while others thicken the sauce so that very little liquid remains. This *khoresht* can be made with lamb or beef.

Preparation

Wash the spinach leaves and dry them in a salad spinner. Cut off and discard any tough stalks; chop the leaves finely with a sharp knife.

Wash the lamb or beef and dry on kitchen paper. Trim off any skin and fat, and cut the meat into 3–4 cm/1½ inch cubes.

Peel and chop both onions, keeping them separate.

Cooking

Heat 30 g/1 oz of the butter with 4 tablespoons of the oil in a medium-sized, heavy-based saucepan. Fry the chopped medium onion until golden brown.

Add the meat and 2 teaspoons of the turmeric, the powdered lime and tomato purée/tomato paste. Season with salt and pepper. Stir to brown the meat lightly on all sides.

Add the boiling water and reduce the heat. Cover with a lid and simmer on a low heat for about 1 hour or until the meat is

Ingredients

1 kg/2¼ lb medium-sized spinach leaves

400 g/14 oz stewing lamb or beef

1 medium onion

1 small onion

50 g/2 oz butter

8 tablespoons vegetable oil

3 teaspoons turmeric

1 heaped tablespoon powdered dried lime (p. 21)

1 heaped teaspoon tomato purée/tomato paste

salt and black pepper

600 ml/1 pint boiling water

200 g/7 oz pitted prunes

3–4 tablespoons lemon juice

2 heaped tablespoons sugar

cooked: it should be tender enough to cut with a fork.

While the meat is cooking, fry the chopped small onion in the remaining 4 tablespoons of oil in a frying pan/skillet until golden brown.

Add the chopped spinach and fry for 5 minutes until the spinach has reduced in volume to about a third and is mixed with the fried onions. Add the remaining 1 teaspoon of turmeric, plus salt and pepper to taste.

Stir the spinach mixture into the meat sauce, which should have reduced to almost half its original volume (about 400 ml/ 14 fl oz). Add the prunes, lemon juice and sugar. Cover and simmer gently for another 30 minutes, or until the sauce is thickened.

Add the remaining butter and mix well. The *khoresht* should have a subtle sweet and sour taste; you may wish to add a little more lemon juice. Turn off heat and replace lid. Allow to stand for up to 30 minutes to let the flavours infuse and the *khoresht* settle.

Serve in a shallow bowl with a dish of plain rice (*chelo*).

TIP: Medium-sized spinach leaves are important in this recipe. Baby leaves will not withstand the length of the cooking process, and large leaves will not have sufficient flavour.

OPPOSITE

Khoresht-e aloo esfenaj is a delicious blend of spinach and prunes enhanced with flavoursome lamb meat.

Aubergine and lamb *khoresht*
Khoresht-e badenjan

Aubergine/eggplant (*badenjan*) is a very popular vegetable in Iran, and this *khoresht* is one of the most traditional ways of using it. There are different varieties of aubergine and the thin, long variety is better for a *khoresht* (rather than the shorter, rounder type, which is preferable for stuffing).

Some regional variations of this recipe include split peas, while others replace lamb with chicken. Sour grapes or verjuice (the juice of green, unripe grapes, which lend the *khoresht* a tart, delicate taste) are popular additions. Tomatoes and tomato purée/tomato paste are not used in very traditional versions.

Remember that aubergine absorbs a lot of oil while frying and can make the whole dish oily. Leave the fried aubergines on sheets of kitchen paper to absorb as much of the oil as possible. Older recipes suggest brushing the aubergine slices with beaten egg white, or brushing them lightly with yogurt, to prevent them from absorbing too much oil. Using a non-stick frying pan/skillet means that you will need less oil. You could also deep-fry the aubergines and drain on plenty of kitchen paper.

Preparation
Peel the aubergines/eggplants and cut each one lengthwise into three slices. Spread them on a large plate, sprinkle with 1 teaspoon of salt and leave to stand for about 15 minutes. Pat dry on kitchen paper.

Wash the lamb and dry on kitchen paper. Trim off any skin and fat, and cut the meat into 3–4 cm/1½ inch cubes.

Peel and finely chop the onion. Wash and dry the tomatoes

Serves 4–6
Preparation: 30 minutes
Cooking: approximately 2 hours, plus standing time

Ingredients
3 medium aubergines/eggplants
salt and black pepper
500 g/1 lb 2 oz lean leg of lamb
1 medium onion
3 beef tomatoes
3 dried limes (p. 21)
approximately 150 ml/5 fl oz vegetable oil
2 teaspoons turmeric
400 g/14 oz canned chopped tomatoes
1 heaped tablespoon tomato purée/tomato paste
1 litre/1¾ pints boiling water
3 tablespoons lemon juice (or verjuice (p. 32)
2 tablespoons liquid saffron (p. 28)

OPPOSITE
Khoresht-e badenjan is a sumptuous feast of aubergine, tomatoes, lamb and sour grapes enhanced with saffron.

OPPOSITE

The khoresht-e badenjan is allowed to stand in the pan for 10-15 minutes before serving.

and cut each into four slices. Wash and dry the dried limes and pierce them with a fork.

Cooking

Heat 4 tablespoons of oil in a medium-sized, heavy-based saucepan and fry the onion until golden brown.

Add the lamb, turmeric, salt and pepper and then the dried limes. Stir until the meat is well coated with the turmeric and sealed all over.

Add the canned chopped tomatoes, tomato purée/tomato paste and boiling water and half-cover the pan with a lid. Simmer on a low heat until the meat is tender enough to cut with a fork and the sauce has reduced to around 500 ml/just under 1 pint; this will take approximately 1–1½ hours.

While the meat is cooking, fry the aubergines until golden brown, preferably in a non-stick frying pan/skillet (if you use an ordinary frying pan, you may need more oil). Remove and pat dry on kitchen paper to remove excess oil.

In the same pan, heat 1 tablespoon of oil and lightly fry the sliced tomatoes. Return the aubergine slices to the frying pan/skillet and turn off the heat. Pour half of the lemon juice and half of the liquid saffron over the aubergine and tomato slices. Set aside.

When the meat is cooked, carefully arrange the aubergine and tomato slices in the sauce on top of the meat. Reduce the heat to very low and let the mixture simmer very gently for about 15 minutes. (The aubergine and tomatoes will disintegrate if the sauce boils vigorously.)

TIPS: Try to keep the aubergine and tomato slices on top of the meat in the saucepan. This makes it easier to transfer them intact into the serving dish.

You can use a mixture of cherry tomatoes and beef tomatoes. For 1 beef tomato use 5 cherry tomatoes.

Add the rest of the lemon juice, salt and pepper to taste. Remove from the heat and leave to stand for 10–15 minutes before serving.

Place in a large shallow bowl, arranging the aubergines and tomatoes over the meat. Pour the remaining liquid saffron over the top. Serve with plain rice (*chelo*).

Serves 6–8
Preparation: 40 minutes
Cooking: approximately
1¾ hours

Ingredients

350 g/12 oz okra

300 g/11 oz potatoes

1 medium onion

4 large cloves of garlic

1–2 dried or fresh chillies

400 g/14 oz leg of lamb

3 tablespoons vegetable oil

1 heaped teaspoon turmeric

salt and black pepper

400 g/14 oz canned chopped
tomatoes

750 ml/1¼ pints boiling water

100 g/3½ oz tamarind paste
dissolved in 200 ml/7 fl oz
boiling water, then strained
(p. 29)

1 tablespoon tomato purée/
tomato paste

3 tablespoons lemon juice
(optional)

Okra and lamb *khoresht*

Khoresht-e bamiyeh

Okra and lamb *khoresht* is cooked throughout Iran, and recipes vary in different regions. This version, from the south, is quite garlicky and spicy, and uses tamarind juice; the okra is cooked until soft and potatoes are added for texture and taste.

Preparation

Cut off the top stems of the okra, taking care not to bruise them, and wash thoroughly. Wash and peel the potatoes and cut them into 4–5 cm/1½–2 inch cubes. Peel and finely chop the onion.

Peel and chop the garlic cloves. Deseed and chop the chillies. Using a pestle and mortar, crush the garlic and chilli together until mixed to a paste.

Wash the lamb and dry it on kitchen paper. Trim off any skin and fat, and cut the meat into 4–5 cm/1½–2 inch cubes.

Cooking

Heat the oil in a medium-sized, heavy-based saucepan and fry the onion until golden. Add the garlic and chilli paste and stir for a couple of minutes.

Add the lamb, turmeric, salt and pepper to the pan. Mix well and fry lightly to seal the meat on all sides.

Add the chopped tomatoes, boiling water and half of the tamarind liquid. Mix thoroughly. Reduce the heat, cover and simmer gently for 1 hour or until the meat is cooked: it should be tender enough to cut with a fork.

Stir in the tomato purée/tomato paste and the potatoes.

Cook for a further 15 minutes or until the potatoes are tender but not falling apart. Add more water if necessary. The liquid should now be reduced to about 500 ml/just under 1 pint.

Add the okra to the pan and pour in the rest of the tamarind liquid. Cover and simmer for 20–30 minutes on a low heat until the okra is soft. Taste and adjust the seasoning, and add lemon juice if you prefer a tarter flavour.

Serve in a shallow bowl with the meat at the bottom and the okra and potatoes arranged on top. Serve with plain rice (*chelo*).

Left: *Animals are reared on open pastures.*

Serves 4–6
Preparation: approximately
20 minutes
Cooking: approximately
1 ½ hours

Ingredients

1 chicken, about 1.8 kg/4 lb
1 medium onion
250 g/9 oz shelled walnuts
3 tablespoons vegetable oil
500 ml/just under 1 pint
chicken stock
350 ml/12 fl oz *robb-e anar*
(pomegranate syrup, p. 24)
4 tablespoons sugar
50 g/2 oz butter

Chicken *khoresht* with walnuts and pomegranates

Khoresht-e fesenjan

Traditionally made with duck, this dish also works well with chicken or lamb. In the north of Iran it is sometimes made with fish. It is a relatively easy *khoresht* to make, but it must be cooked slowly to allow the flavours to develop in the sauce. The consistency should be thick and creamy and the colour almost black. The distinctive flavour combines the nutty taste of ground walnuts with the sweet and sour flavour of pomegranate syrup.

Preparation

Wash and dry the chicken, and remove the skin.

Peel and finely chop the onion.

Grind the walnuts in a food processor, or crush them in a pestle and mortar.

Cooking

Heat half of the oil in a large, heavy-based saucepan. Seal the chicken on all sides. Remove the chicken from the pan and fry the onion in the remaining oil until golden.

Add the ground walnuts, stock, pomegranate syrup and sugar. Stir well and reduce the heat.

Put the chicken back in the pan, cover and simmer on a low heat until the chicken is cooked (approximately 45–50 minutes): the flesh should start to come away from the bones.

Take the chicken out of the sauce, put it in a bowl, cover and keep warm. Continue to simmer the liquid on a low heat for a further 10–15 minutes to reduce the sauce until a thin film of oil from the walnuts forms on top and the sauce turns a dark chocolate brown colour.

Return the chicken to the pan and add the butter. Cover and simmer gently for a further 10 minutes. To serve, take the chicken out and place in a serving bowl, stir the sauce well and pour over the chicken.

This dish is traditionally served with plain rice (*chelo*), but I also serve it with Saffron barberry rice (*Zereshk polo*, p. 164), which is very popular with my friends in the West, though most Iranians would find this unusual.

Below: The rich taste of Khoresht-e fesenjan requires plain rice to offset the glorious flavours.

Serves 4
Preparation: approximately
30 minutes
Cooking: approximately 1 hour

Ingredients

1 large lemon
4 chicken pieces (breast or
thigh), (or 2 whole poussins)
salt and black pepper
500 g/1 lb 2 oz mushrooms
1 medium onion
50 g/2 oz butter
3 tablespoons vegetable oil
1 teaspoon turmeric
2 tablespoons liquid saffron
(p. 28)
500 ml/just under 1 pint chicken
stock
1 teaspoon tomato purée/tomato
paste

Chicken *khoresht* with saffron and mushrooms

Khoresht-e gharch

This is an easy dish to prepare. You can use cultivated or wild mushrooms, but 'beefier' types, such as chestnut, work best. Wild mushrooms such as porcini are more aromatic and will give a stronger taste.

Preparation

Cut the lemon in half and squeeze one half: you should have about 2 tablespoons of juice; set aside.

Remove the chicken skin, wash the pieces and pat dry on kitchen paper. Put the chicken in a bowl, rub with the unsqueezed half lemon and squeeze the juice over them. Sprinkle with salt and pepper; set aside.

Clean the mushrooms by wiping them with damp kitchen paper, then slice them thickly. Chop the onion finely.

Cooking

Heat half of the butter with half of the oil in a medium-sized, heavy-based saucepan. Fry the onion until lightly golden.

Add the chicken pieces or poussins to the pan (reserve the lemon juice you have squeezed over them), followed by the turmeric. Fry until golden on all sides.

Add 2 teaspoons of the liquid saffron, the reserved lemon juice you squeezed over the chicken, and the stock. Cover with a lid, reduce the heat to low and simmer for approximately 30 minutes or until the chicken is cooked; the flesh should start to come off the bones. The sauce should be reduced to half its original volume, approximately 250 ml/9 fl oz. If there is too much liquid, remove the chicken and increase the heat to reduce the sauce; it should be quite thick.

Meanwhile, heat the remaining butter and oil in a frying pan/skillet and sauté the sliced mushrooms. You will probably need to do this in batches: do not overload the pan or the mushrooms will release too much liquid and will poach rather than sauté. Take care not to overcook them. Remove from the heat. Add 2 tablespoons of lemon juice and 2 teaspoons of liquid saffron and stir gently to coat the mushrooms.

Add the mushrooms to the pan with the chicken and its sauce. Add the tomato purée/tomato paste, stir well and simmer for 10–15 minutes. Before serving add the remaining 2 teaspoons liquid saffron. Taste and add more lemon juice, salt or pepper if desired. Serve with plain rice (*chelo*).

VARIATION

Khoresht-e gharch makes a tasty vegetarian dish: leave out the chicken and use vegetable stock (or dissolve 2 vegetable stock cubes in 500 ml/just under 1 pint of boiling water) instead of chicken stock. Leave out the saffron and lemon juice added to the chicken. Add the turmeric to the chopped onion as you fry it. Cook the mushrooms as above. Add the mushrooms and tomato purée/tomato paste and simmer for 20–30 minutes to thicken the sauce. Just before serving, add 2 teaspoons of liquid saffron.

Khoresht of fish with coriander
Ghalyeh mahi

Ghalyeh comes from the southern provinces of Iran, where it is made with fish such as red snapper or *hamoor* or with prawns/shrimp (see variation). In the West, fish such as sea bream, cod or monkfish can be used.

Ghalyeh also has local variations. In Bushehr on the Persian Gulf, where it is a very popular dish, the fish head and tail are added to the sauce to give a thicker consistency and a richer taste. More chillies are added, too, for a hot and spicy result.

This is a relatively straightforward dish to make, but it must be cooked very slowly to let the flavour develop.

Preparation

Wash the coriander/cilantro and dry it in a salad spinner or a clean tea towel. Pick off the fresh green leaves and tender stalks, discarding the rest. Finely chop the leaves and stalks with a sharp, wide-bladed knife.

Peel and finely chop the onion and garlic. Top and tail the chillies, then chop finely. Using a pestle and mortar, crush the garlic and chilli together until mixed to a paste.

Clean the fish, wash, pat dry on kitchen paper and cut into large chunks – or ask your fishmonger to prepare the fish for you. Using the head and tail of the fish is optional; they will give the *ghalyeh* a richer consistency and fishy flavour.

Cooking

Heat the oil and the butter in a medium-sized, heavy-based saucepan and fry the onion until golden. Add the crushed garlic

Serves 4–6
Preparation: approximately
45 minutes
Cooking: approximately
1 1/4 hours

Ingredients

250 g/9 oz fresh coriander/cilantro
1 large onion
5 cloves of garlic
1 or 2 fresh chillies (more if you like a spicier taste)
750 g/1 lb 10 oz chunky fish fillet such as sea bream, cod or monkfish, including the head and tail if you like
4 tablespoons sunflower oil
30 g/1 oz butter
2 teaspoons turmeric
2 tablespoons plain/all-purpose flour
3 tablespoons dried fenugreek
100 g/3 1/2 oz tamarind paste dissolved in 500 ml/just under 1 pint boiling water, then strained (p. 29)
salt and black pepper

OPPOSITE
Ghalyeh mahi, a spicy fish dish made with coriander and fenugreek in a thick tamarind sauce.

To make *Ghalyeh maygoo* (Prawn *ghalyeh*), replace the fish with 750 g/1 lb 10 oz of large prawns/shrimp. Wash and peel the prawns, removing the heads but leaving the tails on. If you are using raw prawns, cut out the black veins from the back of the prawns.

Make as for fish *ghalyeh*: add the prawns/shrimp to the thickened sauce and simmer on a low heat for no more than 10–15 minutes.

and chilli paste, turmeric and flour. Stir well. Add the coriander/cilantro and fenugreek and fry for a further 3–4 minutes.

Add the tamarind liquid; season with salt and pepper to taste. Reduce the heat and simmer very gently, uncovered, for 30–40 minutes until the sauce is thick.

When the sauce has thickened add the fish, piece by piece (including the head and tail if using). Simmer very gently on a low heat for another 30 minutes until the fish is cooked. Take care not to overcook the fish; the pieces should not disintegrate when you serve them.

Remove the fish from the pan (discarding the head and tail if you prefer). Place the fish in a shallow bowl and pour the sauce all around. *Ghalyeh* is usually served with plain rice (*chelo*) or flat bread.

Lamb *khoresht* with split peas and fried potatoes

Khoresht-e gheimeh

Before the introduction of electric fridges, families in the colder, northern provinces of Iran such as Azerbaijan devised ingenious ways to preserve meat for consumption during the winter months. The meat would be cut into small pieces (*gheimeh*), fried with onions, flavoured with turmeric and other spices and put into big earthenware vats. A thick layer of solidified fat on the top ensures a good seal against micro-organisms. These vats were kept in dark, cold basements over the winter. Each day, a small amount would be taken to add to the *khoresht*.

Khoresht-e gheimeh is diced meat combined with yellow split peas, dried limes and saffron with fried potatoes. It is very popular all over Iran and can be cooked all year round; the combination of meat and pulses, served with rice, provides a nutritious meal.

Preparation

Wash and soak the split peas in cold water for at least 30 minutes or overnight (follow the instructions on the packet).

Peel and chop the onion. Wash and dry the dried limes and pierce with a fork.

Wash and dry the lamb, trim off any skin and fat and cut the meat into 1 cm/½ inch cubes.

Cooking

Heat the butter and oil in a medium-sized, heavy-based saucepan. Fry the onion until golden.

Serves 4
Preparation: 30 minutes, plus soaking
Cooking: approximately 1½ hours

Ingredients

100 g/3½ oz yellow split peas
1 medium onion
4 dried limes (p. 21)
300 g/11 oz leg of lamb
50 g/2 oz butter
4 tablespoons vegetable oil
2 teaspoons turmeric
2 teaspoons powdered dried lime (p. 21)
salt and black pepper
1 litre/1¾ pints boiling water
1 tablespoon tomato purée/ tomato paste
2 tablespoons lemon juice
2 tablespoons liquid saffron (p. 28)

Garnish

2 medium potatoes
vegetable oil for deep frying
30 g/1 oz mixed pistachios and almonds

Add the lamb, turmeric, lime powder, whole dried limes, salt and pepper. Stir well and fry until the meat is golden brown all over.

Add the boiling water and reduce the heat. Cover with a lid and simmer on a low heat until the meat is cooked (approximately 45 minutes to 1 hour): it should be tender enough to cut with a fork.

Drain the split peas and add to the pan. Cover and cook on a low heat for about 20–30 minutes or until the split peas are cooked: they should be soft while still retaining their shape. Add small amounts of boiling water if the mixture looks dry.

Add the tomato purée/tomato paste, lemon juice and 1 tablespoon of liquid saffron and cook for a further 10 minutes on a low heat.

Garnish

While the lamb is cooking, peel, wash and dry the potatoes. Cut them into sticks about 3 cm/1¼ inches long and place them in a bowl of cold water to prevent discoloration. Cut the nuts into slivers.

Deep-fry the potatoes in vegetable oil until golden brown. Drain on kitchen paper. Heat 1 tablespoon of oil in a small saucepan. Lightly fry the nuts for a couple of minutes until pale golden. Add the remaining 1 tablespoon of liquid saffron to the nuts and set aside.

Serve the *khoresht* in a shallow dish. Garnish with the fried potato sticks and the nuts.

Khoresht-e gheimeh is normally served with plain rice (*chelo*), but for special occasions can be served with the colourful Saffron jewelled rice (*morassa' polo*, p. 155).

Lamb *khoresht* with red kidney beans and herbs

Khoresht-e ghormeh sabzi

A popular favourite throughout Iran, this is a meal for both festive occasions and family meals. Recipes from different regions vary slightly. The Azerbaijani version, for example, uses black-eyed beans instead of red kidney beans. Recipes in the south of the country add chilli and garlic, while in Shiraz potatoes are sometimes used instead of beans. The recipe here departs from tradition by adding spinach to enhance the taste and give the dish a softer texture. Fenugreek gives a very distinctive aroma and flavour.

Chopping the herbs takes time, but you can cook *ghormeh sabzi* in advance and reheat it gently before serving; the flavour is improved by keeping it in the fridge overnight as the aroma of the herbs diffuses through the sauce.

Preparation

If using dried red kidney beans, wash them and soak them in cold water overnight.

Wash the lamb, pat dry and trim off any skin and fat. Cut the meat into 4–5 cm/1½–2 inch cubes.

Peel and finely chop the onions and garlic. Deseed and finely chop the chilli, if using. Wash and dry the whole dried limes and pierce them a couple of times with a fork.

Wash the spinach, chives, parsley and coriander/cilantro in cold water, discarding any tough stalks and wilting and yellowing leaves. Dry the leaves and tender stalks in a salad spinner or

Serves 4–6
Preparation: approximately
1 hour, plus optional soaking
Cooking: approximately 2 hours,
plus standing time

Ingredients

250 g/9 oz canned red kidney beans (drained weight), (or 150 g/5 oz dried red kidney beans)

500 g/1 lb 2 oz lean leg of lamb

2 medium onions

4 cloves of garlic

1 small chilli (optional)

5 dried limes (p. 21)

150 g/5 oz spinach

100 g/3½ oz chives

150g/5 oz parsley

100 g/3½ oz fresh coriander/cilantro

4–5 tablespoons vegetable oil

2 teaspoons turmeric

1 litre/1¾ pints boiling water

4 tablespoons dried fenugreek

2 tablespoons powdered dried lime (p. 21)

salt and black pepper

juice of 1 lemon (optional)

30 g/1 oz butter

a clean tea towel. Finely chop the herbs using a sharp, wide-bladed knife.

Cooking

Heat 2 tablespoons of the oil in a medium-sized, heavy-based saucepan. Fry half of the chopped onions until golden.

Add the lamb, turmeric, half of the chopped garlic and two of the dried limes. Mix thoroughly and fry the meat until lightly brown and sealed on all sides. If you are using dried kidney beans, drain them and add to the pan after the lamb has browned.

Add the boiling water, reduce the heat to low and cover with a lid. Simmer for 1 hour or until the meat is nearly cooked: it should be tender enough to cut with a fork. You should have about 500 ml/just under 1 pint of liquid left in the pan. If necessary, continue to simmer and reduce the stock further.

While the meat is cooking, heat 2 tablespoons of oil in a large frying pan/skillet and fry the rest of the onion. Add the rest of the garlic and the chilli, if using, and stir well. Fold in the chopped herbs and the fenugreek. Add the powdered lime and fry gently for 5–10 minutes until the herbs shrink in volume and are well mixed with the onion, garlic and chilli. If the herbs start to stick to the pan, add another tablespoon of oil.

Stir the remaining dried whole limes and the fried herb mixture into the lamb. If you are using canned kidney beans, add them at this stage. Cover with a lid and simmer on a very low heat for 45 minutes. Taste and adjust the seasoning, adding lemon juice if you like, and simmer for a further 5 minutes. Stir in the butter.

Take the pan off the heat and leave to stand for 15–30 minutes before serving so the flavours can permeate the sauce. Stir well and serve in a shallow bowl, accompanied by plain rice.

VARIATION

You can make *Khoresht-e ghormeh sabzi* without meat. Fry the chopped onions, all the garlic and the chilli with the turmeric until the onion is golden. Add the kidney beans (if you are using soaked dried beans), chopped herbs, fenugreek and dried lime powder and fry for 5–10 minutes until the herbs shrink in volume.

Add 600 ml/1 pint vegetable stock and the dried limes to the herb mixture. Reduce the heat and simmer gently for 1 hour. The sauce should be thick and dark green. Add the canned kidney beans, lemon juice and seasoning to taste. Simmer for another 20 minutes. Leave to stand, off the heat, for 20–30 minutes before serving.

OPPOSITE

Koresht-e ghormeh sabzi is a firm favourite in Iran, at family dinners and celebrations alike.

Serves 4–6
Preparation: approximately
45 minutes
Cooking: approximately 2 hours

Ingredients

500 g/1lb 2 oz lean leg of lamb
400 g/14 oz fresh herbs: 200 g/
7 oz parsley, 150 g/5 oz coriander/
cilantro, 50 g/2 oz mint
350 g/12 oz young celery sticks
2 medium onions
100 ml/3½ fl oz sunflower oil
2 teaspoons turmeric
salt and black pepper
500 ml/just under 1 pint boiling
water
1 tablespoon tomato purée/
tomato paste
50 g/2 oz butter
3 tablespoons lemon juice (the
juice of 1 large lemon)

Lamb *khoresht* with celery and herbs

Khoresht-e karafs

Aromatic herbs and lemon juice give a piquant taste to the cooked celery in this fresh-tasting dish. Celery comes into its own when cooked with parsley, coriander and mint.

Preparation

Wash the lamb and dry on kitchen paper. Trim off any skin and fat, and cut the meat into 3–4 cm/1½ inch cubes.

Wash the herbs in cold water and dry them in a salad spinner or a clean tea towel. Discard any wilting or yellow leaves and tough stalks, then chop the herbs finely with a sharp, wide-bladed knife. You can chop the herbs while the lamb is cooking or prepare them up to 24 hours in advance: place in a bowl, cover with a damp cloth and keep in the fridge.

Wash the celery in cold water, pat dry and cut into 2–3 cm/ approximately 1 inch pieces. Chop the onions.

Cooking

Heat half of the oil in a large, heavy-based saucepan, add half of the chopped onions and fry until golden. Add the lamb and turmeric. Stir well to coat the lamb in oil and turmeric and fry until the lamb is golden brown.

Add salt and pepper, and then the boiling water. Bring back to the boil, then reduce the heat and simmer gently for 1–1¼ hours until the meat is cooked: it should be tender enough to cut with a fork.

Heat the remaining oil in a deep frying pan/skillet, large enough to hold all the herbs and celery. Fry the remaining onion until golden.

Add the celery and fry, stirring, until golden brown on the edges. Remove the celery and onion mixture from the pan with a slotted spoon and add to the lamb.

Add the chopped herbs to the frying pan/skillet and fry gently for 5 minutes. The herbs will shrink alarmingly in volume, but all their flavours are captured.

Add the fried herbs to the lamb mixture and stir well. Add the tomato purée/tomato paste and butter and let it simmer gently on a low heat for 30–40 minutes, until the sauce is thick and aromatic.

Add the lemon juice and adjust the seasoning to taste.

Turn off heat and replace lid. Allow to stand for up to 30 minutes to let the flavours infuse and the *khoresht* settle.

Serve with plain rice (*chelo*).

✵

Lamb and potato *khoresht* with tamarind

Khoresht-e seebzamini

The delicious combination of red lentils and potato with rich tomato sauce makes *Khoresht-e seebzamini* very popular in the south of Iran. There are several local variations. In Bushehr on the Persian Gulf, for example, it is very spicy, with lots of chillies and garlic.

Preparation

Wash the lamb, pat dry and trim off any skin and fat. Cut the meat into 4–5 cm/1½–2 inch cubes.

Peel the onion and chop finely. Peel the garlic, deseed and chop the chilli; using a pestle and mortar, crush the garlic and chilli together until mixed to a paste.

Wash the lentils in several changes of cold water, then drain. Peel the potatoes and cut each one in half. Place them in a bowl of cold water to prevent discoloration.

Cooking

Heat the oil in a large, heavy-based saucepan and fry the onion until golden. Add the crushed garlic and chilli paste and turmeric and stir well. Fry for 1 minute.

Add the lamb and lentils and mix thoroughly. Fry for 3–4 minutes.

Add the chopped tomatoes and stir well. Add the boiling water and bring the mixture to the boil. Cover and simmer on a low heat for 1 hour or until the lamb is cooked: it should be tender

Serves 4–6
Preparation: approximately
30 minutes
Cooking: approximately
1¾ hours

Ingredients
400 g/14 oz lean leg of lamb
1 medium onion
6 cloves of garlic
1 fresh chilli
30 g/1 oz red lentils
300 g/11 oz waxy salad potatoes
3 tablespoons vegetable oil
1 teaspoon turmeric
400 g/14 oz canned chopped tomatoes
600 ml/1 pint boiling water
30 g/1 oz tamarind paste dissolved in 100 ml/3½ fl oz boiling water, then strained (p. 29)
2 tablespoons tomato purée/ tomato paste
salt and black pepper
juice of 1 lemon (optional)

OPPOSITE
Khoresht-e seebzamini is a hearty and spicy dish delicious all year round.

VARIATION

To make a vegetarian version of *Khoresht-e seebzamini*: fry the onion, garlic, chilli and turmeric. Add the potatoes, red lentils, chopped tomatoes, tomato purée/ tomato paste and 500 ml/just under 1 pint vegetable stock (or 2 vegetable stock cubes dissolved in 500 ml boiling water). Cover and simmer gently for approximately 40 minutes, until the sauce thickens and the potatoes are cooked.

Add the tamarind liquid and stir well. Leave to simmer for a further 10 minutes. Season to taste. Add the juice of 1 lemon for a more piquant sauce.

enough to cut with a fork. The liquid should have reduced to about 300 ml/10 fl oz by this stage. If not, continue to simmer for a few more minutes.

Drain the potatoes and add them to the pan, together with the tamarind liquid and tomato purée/tomato paste. Taste and adjust the seasoning, and add the lemon juice if you prefer a tarter flavour.

Cover and simmer for a further 30 minutes or until the potatoes are soft when pierced with a fork, but retaining their shape. Take care not to overcook the potatoes.
If you have time, leave the khoresht to rest for up to 30 minutes to allow the flavours to develop fully.

Serve in a shallow dish accompanied by plain rice (*chelo*).

OPPOSITE

Beautiful mosaic detail from the dome of a mosque.

Chapter 4

KHORAKS, KABABS AND KOOFTEHS

Chapter 4

Khoraks, kababs, kooftehs and other main dishes

OPPOSITE

Top: Roast poussin (Joojeh
tanoori, p. 96).

Bottom: Koofteh ghelgheli (p. 108)
served with rice and tahdig.

*K*horak is literally the Persian word for food, but in culinary terms it has come to represent a miscellany of dishes: meat, chicken, fish or vegetarian dishes which may be roasted, grilled/broiled, fried or stewed but always with only a small amount of sauce – or in some cases without any sauce at all. They are usually eaten on informal family occasions and, unlike *khoreshts*, are not necessarily served with rice.

Kababs, or kebabs, are basically skewers of grilled meat cooked over charcoal. Although a simple dish to prepare and cook, *kababs* stand or fall on the quality of the meat and the marinade. Whether you use beef or lamb, the most tender part – the fillet – is used. The meat is left for a couple of hours or longer to absorb the tastes and aromas of the ingredients in the marinade. It is then threaded onto flat skewers and grilled for a short period of time over intense heat to keep the meat deliciously juicy. You can cook kebabs on a hot barbecue or under the grill in your kitchen. They are served with flat bread or, more often, with rice. *Chelo kabab*, skewers of lamb served with rice, is often described as Iran's national dish.

Koofteh (meatballs) is an old Persian dish that is very popular all over Iran. Traditionally the meat was pounded in a stone mortar and pestle and then mixed with rice and other ingredients. There are many versions of *koofteh*, from a simple combination

of minced/ground meat with grated onion to more elaborately spiced or herb-flavoured mixtures. They can be served with rice dishes, potatoes or flat bread and salad.

Other traditional main dishes include *kotlets* (fried meat patties or rissoles), *dolmeh* (stuffed vegetables) and *kookoo*, which is often translated as 'omelette', although it more closely resembles a Spanish tortilla: the eggs are combined with herbs and vegetables and cooked slowly. These dishes can be made in advance and eaten over a couple of days. Because they have no sauce (or very little sauce in the case of *dolmeh*) they can be packed for picnics or used as a sandwich filling. On formal occasions these dishes are thought of as fillers; you would have one or two *khoreshts* with a plain white rice and a *polo* as the main feature and a couple of dishes of this sort to fill the *sofreh* along with salads, fresh herbs (*Sabzi khordan*, p. 17) and a yogurt-based dish.

Right: *Stuffed pepper (see Dolmeh, p. 119).*

Saffron yogurt lamb

Barreh za'farani

Lamb shanks have an almost legendary reputation in Persian cuisine for fortifying and restoring strength, especially after an illness. Traditionally, they are simply simmered in water until almost dry, then put in the middle of a rice dish and steamed. This recipe gives a more aromatic result, with succulent meat cooked separately. It can be served with various rice dishes (see Chapter 5), such as *Baghala polo*, *Adas polo*, *Zereshk polo* and *Sabzi polo*.

Preparation

Wash the lamb shanks and dry on kitchen paper. Trim off any excess fat.

Wash and dry the dried limes and pierce them with a fork. If you are using fresh lime, grate the zest and squeeze the juice.

Peel the onion and cut it into four chunky pieces. Peel and crush the garlic. In a small bowl, mix the garlic, cumin and coriander seeds to a paste. Rub the garlic and spice mixture over the lamb shanks, rubbing it well into the meat. Season with salt and pepper.

Cooking

In a large, heavy-based saucepan (preferably cast-iron), heat the oil and fry the onion until just golden. Add the lamb shanks and seal all around: they should not be cooked too much, just enough to turn the edges brown. Add the turmeric and the dried limes, or fresh lime zest and juice. Stir to coat the meat in turmeric.

Pour in the stock, cover the pan with a lid, bring to the boil and reduce the heat; simmer gently for 2–2½ hours, until the meat can be easily separated from the bone.

Serves 4–6
Preparation: 25 minutes
Cooking: approximately
3 hours

Ingredients
4 lamb shanks
4 dried limes (p. 21),
(or 1 fresh lime)
1 large onion
4 cloves of garlic
1 teaspoon ground cumin
1 teaspoon ground coriander
seeds
salt and black pepper
2 tablespoons vegetable oil
2 teaspoons turmeric
600 ml/1 pint chicken stock
4 heaped tablespoons Greek-
style full-fat/whole milk yogurt
1 tablespoon lemon juice
2 tablespoons liquid saffron
(p. 28)
sprigs of mint to decorate

Above: *The inclusion of yogurt in Barreh za'farani brings a rich texture and subtle flavour to the lamb.*

TIP: Leg or shoulder of lamb can be used instead of shanks if preferred. The shoulder cooks more quickly, is cheaper and more flavoursome but is more fatty.

Take the shanks out of the pan and transfer to a large bowl; cover with a lid to keep them warm. Simmer the sauce to reduce to about 100 ml/3½ fl oz and then remove from the heat.

Mix the yogurt with the lemon juice and liquid saffron. Pour half of the yogurt mixture over the shanks and the rest into the reduced juice in the pan. Return the shanks to the pan (off the heat) and put the lid on. Reheat gently; make sure that you don't bring the sauce to the boil as the yogurt will separate. Taste and adjust the seasoning.

To serve, arrange the shanks in a shallow dish and pour the juice around. Decorate with a few sprigs of mint.

Lamb shanks in tomato sauce
Khorak-e mahicheh

Lamb shanks must be cooked slowly, to keep the meat moist and tender. This recipe is very easy to prepare and cook. It can be served with Cumin saffron rice (*Zireh polo*, p. 167) or flat bread, but is equally good with mashed potato.

Preparation

Wash and dry the lamb shanks. Trim off any excess fat. Grate the lemon zest and squeeze the juice. Peel the onion and cut it into four or six wedges. Peel and crush the garlic. Rub the shanks all over with the crushed garlic, lemon zest, salt and pepper.

To prepare the garnish, wash and dry the parsley and finely chop the leaves. Finely chop the lemon and lime halves, including the skin. Peel and finely chop the garlic. Mix all the garnish ingredients together and season with salt and pepper.

Cooking

In a large, heavy-based saucepan, heat the oil and fry the onion until just golden. Add the lamb shanks and turmeric. Stir until the meat is well coated with the turmeric and sealed all over.

Add the chopped tomatoes, tomato purée and the stock. Mix thoroughly, bring to the boil and then reduce the heat, cover the pan with a lid and simmer gently for 2–2½ hours, until the meat can be easily separated from the bone. Once the meat is cooked, remove the lamb shanks from the pan with a slotted spoon. Simmer the sauce to reduce to about 125 ml/4 fl oz. Put the shanks back in the sauce and add the lemon juice. Taste and adjust the seasoning.

To serve, arrange the lamb shanks in a shallow dish and sprinkle the garnish over them.

Serves 4
Preparation: 30 minutes
Cooking: approximately 3 hours

Ingredients

4 small lamb shanks
1 medium lemon
1 large onion
6 cloves of garlic
salt and black pepper
3 tablespoons vegetable oil
2 teaspoons turmeric
400 g/14 oz canned chopped tomatoes
2 heaped tablespoons tomato purée/tomato paste
500 ml/just under 1 pint vegetable stock

Garnish

15 g/½ oz parsley
½ lemon and ½ lime
1 clove of garlic

Serves 4–6
Preparation: 20 minutes
*Cooking: 45–50 minutes, plus
standing time*

Ingredients

2 poussins (at room temperature)
2 medium potatoes
2 large cloves of garlic
1 lemon
2 teaspoons mustard (any type)
4 tablespoons extra virgin
olive oil
2 tablespoons liquid saffron
(p. 28)
salt and black pepper
30 g/1 oz butter

Roast poussin

Joojeh tanoori

Poussins are very young chickens, which are tasty and tender. You can use small free-range chickens instead.

Preparation

Preheat the oven to 200°C/400°F/gas mark 6.

Wash and dry the poussins and strip off any excess skin and fat. Peel the potatoes and cut into wedges. Peel and crush the garlic. Grate the lemon zest and squeeze the juice; reserve the squeezed lemon halves.

In a bowl mix the mustard, crushed garlic, olive oil, lemon zest and juice and the liquid saffron.

Rub the poussins with salt and pepper and the squeezed lemon halves. Gently ease your fingers between the skin and the breast of the poussins, then rub the birds inside and out and under the skin with the mustard mixture.

Cooking

Place the poussins in a roasting pan. Dot with butter and arrange the potato wedges around them. Roast in the oven for 45–50 minutes. Turn the birds after about 25 minutes.

When the poussins are cooked, remove from the oven and allow to stand for 10 minutes.

Arrange the poussins and potatoes in a serving dish and pour any pan juices over the poussins.

See p. 91 for recipe image.

Saffron lemon chicken

Joojeh za'farani

Although easy to prepare, the combination of tangy lemon and heady saffron lends this recipe a degree of sophistication fit for any occasion. It goes well with most rice dishes that don't include chicken or meat, and particularly with Saffron barberry rice (*Zereshk polo*, p. 164).

Preparation

Skin and wash the chicken pieces or the poussins. Grate the lemon zest and squeeze the juice. Rub the chicken or poussin with the zest and half the juice of the lemon. Season with salt and black pepper.

Peel the onion and cut it into four pieces. Peel and finely chop the garlic.

Cooking

Heat the butter with the oil in a medium-sized, heavy-based saucepan on a medium heat. Fry the onion until lightly golden. Add the garlic, stir, then add the chicken pieces or poussins and fry until golden on all sides.

Add half of the liquid saffron, the remaining lemon juice and the stock. Cover with a lid, reduce the heat and simmer for about 30 minutes or until the chicken is cooked. The sauce should be quite thick at this stage; if it is not, simmer to reduce further.

Add the tomato purée/tomato paste, taste and adjust the seasoning and cook for another 5–10 minutes.

Transfer the chicken pieces, or the poussins, to a shallow serving dish, pour over the sauce and the remaining liquid saffron.

Serves 4
Preparation: 20 minutes
Cooking: 45–50 minutes

Ingredients

8 chicken pieces (legs and breast) or 2 poussins (at room temperature)
1 lemon
salt and black pepper
1 medium onion
2 cloves of garlic
30 g/1 oz butter
2 tablespoons vegetable oil
4 tablespoons liquid saffron (p. 28)
200 ml/7 fl oz chicken stock
1 heaped teaspoon tomato purée/tomato paste

Serves 4–6
Preparation: approximately
25 minutes, plus soaking
Cooking: approximately
1 ½ hours, plus standing time

Ingredients

100 g/3½ oz pitted prunes
100 g/3½ oz dried apricots
juice of 1 medium lemon
5 tablespoons liquid saffron
(p. 28)
1 chicken, about 1.8 kg/4 lb (at
room temperature)
1 medium onion
1 medium orange, preferably
unwaxed
2 tablespoons vegetable oil
2 tablespoons butter
1 teaspoon dried tarragon
1 teaspoon ground cumin
salt and black pepper

Roast chicken stuffed with apricots, prunes and orange
Morghe shekampor

Fresh and dried fruits are often used for stuffing poultry – and sometimes shoulder of lamb – in the north of Iran. This recipe uses a combination of dried fruits mixed with orange and tarragon. The stuffing keeps the chicken moist as it roasts and the aroma of orange and tarragon pervades the chicken.

Serve with plain rice (*chelo*) or with Saffron barberry rice (*Zereshk polo*, p. 164), Cumin saffron rice (*Zireh polo*, p. 167) or Herb rice (*Sabzi polo*, p. 159).

Preparation

Cut the prunes and apricots into 1 cm/½ inch pieces. Put them in a small bowl, add half of the lemon juice and 2 tablespoons of the liquid saffron and leave to soak for about 30 minutes.

Wash the chicken and dry it thoroughly. Trim off any excess fat. Peel the onion and chop finely. Wash the orange and pare off the zest. Cut the zest into slivers. Peel off the pith and thinly slice the flesh, discarding the pips.

Cooking

Heat the oil with half of the butter in a large frying pan/skillet and fry the onion until golden. Remove the apricot and the prune pieces from their soaking liquid with a slotted spoon then add to the onion together with the orange slices, stir and fry for a couple of minutes. Add the orange zest, tarragon and cumin, stir, and continue frying for another minute or two. Remove from the heat and let the mixture cool.

Preheat the oven to 220°C/425°F/gas mark 7.

Place the chicken, breast up, in a roasting pan and stuff with the apricot and prune mixture. Pour the remaining lemon juice and liquid saffron over the breast and dot with the rest of the butter. Roast in the middle of the oven for 20 minutes, then turn the chicken over, reduce the oven temperature to 200°C/400°F/gas mark 6 and roast for a further 20 minutes.

Turn the chicken over and continue to roast for 30–35 minutes or until it is cooked and golden. Let it stand for 10 minutes before serving.

Above: Prunes are an important ingredient in many Persian dishes.

Serves 4
Preparation: 30 minutes
Cooking: 25 minutes

Ingredients

4 trout, preferably small rainbow
trout
100 g/3½ oz fresh coriander/
cilantro
1 medium onion
4 cloves of garlic
1 small chilli (add more if you
like it spicy)
1 lemon or lime
salt and black pepper
2 tablespoons vegetable oil, plus
extra for greasing the foil
30 g/1 oz butter
1 teaspoon turmeric
1 teaspoon ground coriander
seeds
1 teaspoon powdered dried lime
(p. 21)
2 tablespoons olive oil

Garnish

slices of lemon
sprigs of herbs

Grilled trout with spicy coriander stuffing

Mahi shekampor

This recipe, from the city of Bushehr in southern Iran, uses a combination of fresh coriander/cilantro, garlic, onion, chilli and powdered dried lime, which really enhances the delicate flavour of the trout. Serve with Herb rice (*Sabzi polo*, p. 159) to create a balanced dish.

Preparation

Wash and dry the trout.

Wash the coriander, dry in a salad spinner and discard any tough stalks. Finely chop the leaves and tender stalks with a sharp, wide-bladed knife.

Peel the onion and garlic and chop finely. Top and tail the chilli. Cut it lengthwise and scrape out the seeds using the blade of a knife. Chop it finely and set aside.

Grate the zest from the lemon or lime, set aside 1 teaspoon of zest and put the rest in the cavity of the fish. Cut the lemon or lime in half, squeeze the juice and set aside. Rub the fish all over with the cut surface of the lemon or lime. Drizzle half of the juice inside the fish and season with salt and pepper.

Cooking

Heat the oil and butter in a frying pan/skillet. Fry the onion until golden brown. Add the garlic, chilli and chopped coriander. Mix in the turmeric, ground coriander, lime powder, salt and pepper. Stir well. Remove from the heat and leave to cool.

Cover a baking sheet with aluminium foil and oil lightly. Preheat the grill/broiler to maximum.

Stuff the trout with the onion and herb mixture and arrange the trout on the baking sheet. Mix the reserved 1 teaspoon of grated zest with the remaining lime or lemon juice, pour over the trout and drizzle with olive oil. Grill the trout for 15 minutes, in the middle of the oven, turning them carefully after about 7 minutes.

Arrange on a serving dish and garnish with slices of lemon and sprigs of herbs.

Above: Hot and spicy coriander stuffing enhances the taste of the trout to perfection. See pp. 88–9 for the finished dish of Mahi shekampor.

Serves 4
Preparation: approximately
15 minutes
Cooking: 10–12 minutes

Ingredients
750 g/1 lb 10 oz cod fillet
50 g/2 oz fresh coriander/
cilantro
2 cloves of garlic
1 small green chilli
1 large lemon
4 tablespoons olive oil, plus
extra for greasing the foil
salt and black pepper

Garnish
slices of lemon (optional)

Cod with coriander

Mahi ba gashneez

This is a very quick and easy dish. Any chunky fish fillet can be used instead of the cod. Serve with Herb rice (*Sabzi polo*, p. 159), Cumin saffron rice (*Zireh polo*, p. 167) or boiled or mashed potato.

Preparation
Wash and dry the fish.

Wash the coriander and dry in a salad spinner. Finely chop the leaves.

Peel the garlic and chop finely. Top and tail the chilli, deseed and finely chop it.

Grate the zest from the lemon and squeeze the juice.

In a shallow bowl mix the garlic, chilli, lemon zest and juice, the olive oil, salt and pepper and half of the chopped coriander. Add the fish and, using your fingers, coat the fish with the mixture.

Cooking
Preheat the grill/broiler to maximum. Cover a baking sheet with aluminium foil and oil lightly.

Arrange the fish fillets side by side on the baking sheet and pour any remaining mixture over them. Put the baking sheet under the grill/broiler, about 10 cm/4 inches away from the heat. Grill for 10–12 minutes or until the fish is lightly golden. Take care not to overcook the fish as it will dry out and lose its flavour.

Serve in a shallow dish and garnish with the remaining coriander and slices of lemon if you like.

Fillet kebab with rice
Chelo kabab barg

If you have been to a Persian restaurant, it is more than likely that you have eaten *chelo kabab*. Skewers of lamb cooked over hot charcoal have been a tradition in Iran for many years. Although *chelo kabab* is basically a skewer or two of barbecued meat with plain rice, a great deal of ritual is involved! Add a knob of butter, the yolk of an egg and a generous sprinkling of sumac (p. 28) to the rice and mix it all together. Eat a piece of grilled tomato, a piece of *kabab* with a spoonful of your rice mixture and experience Persian cuisine at its simplest yet most exquisite. (The method for *chelo* rice is on p. 134.)

Alternatively, have your *kabab* wrapped in freshly baked flat bread with barbecued tomatoes and fresh herbs, eat in or take away.

The traditional *Chelo kabab barg* is made from lamb fillet; I prefer beef, which is unusual in Iran. Some kebabs are made from pounded meat, but *chelo kebab* usually refers to the version made from tender strips of meat. This recipe is easy to prepare and the meat does not need to be grilled over charcoal; it can be cooked under the grill/broiler in the kitchen. Both methods are explained below.

Preparation

Cut the beef fillet lengthwise, along the grain of the meat, into pieces about 8–10 cm/3–4 inches long, 5 cm/2 inches wide and 1 cm/½ inch thick.

Peel and grate the onion. Put the onion, yogurt and 2 teaspoons of the liquid saffron in a shallow bowl and mix thoroughly. Add the pieces of meat and mix to ensure that all the meat is coated

Serves 4
Preparation: approximately 20 minutes, plus marinating
Cooking: approximately 8–10 minutes

Ingredients
800 g/1¾ lb beef fillet
1 medium onion
2 heaped tablespoons Greek-style full-fat/whole milk yogurt
4 teaspoons liquid saffron (p. 28)
2 beef tomatoes
30 g/1 oz butter
sumac powder (p. 28)

with the marinade. Cover the bowl with cling film/plastic wrap and set aside for at least 2 hours, preferably longer, up to 24 hours in the fridge.

Wash the tomatoes and cut in half.

Cooking

Before cooking allow the meat to come to room temperature (if you have kept it in the fridge). Take the meat out of the marinade and use a spatula to scrape off most of the onion. You don't need to be thorough, as the bits of onion add to the flavour when grilled.

Melt the butter and mix in the remaining liquid saffron; set aside.

If you are cooking on a barbecue, make sure it is very hot. Using flat metal skewers, which make it easy to turn the meat over on the barbecue, pierce through the thickness of the pieces of meat. Put the tomato halves on separate skewers to grill alongside the meat. Grill the meat for 3–5 minutes on each side, or less if you like your kebabs rare. Baste the meat with the butter and saffron mixture as it cooks.

If you are cooking in the kitchen, preheat the grill/broiler to maximum. Put the meat and tomato halves on a baking sheet and place very close to the heat – not more than 10 cm/4 inches away. Grill the meat for about 4–5 minutes on each side, basting with the butter and saffron mixture.

Warm a serving dish and arrange the kebabs and the grilled tomatoes on it. Serve with plain rice (*chelo*) and sumac (p. 28).

Chicken kebab

Joojeh kabab

Before the advent of rotisserie chicken in Iran, takeaway shops selling grilled chicken used real barbecues. Along one wall stretched a built-in trough filled with red-hot coals where the chickens, marinated overnight, were grilled as the orders came in. An intense and even heat is required to achieve the desired result.

Preparation

Ask your butcher to spatchcock or 'butterfly' your chickens – but it's not difficult to do this yourself. Put the chicken on a chopping board, breast bone down. Using poultry shears, cut along either side of the backbone and remove it, then turn the chicken over and press down on the breast bone to flatten the chicken. Wash and dry the chickens on kitchen paper.

Using a sharp knife, make a shallow slit through the thigh flesh and a couple of slits through the breast fillets and the back. This will let the marinade penetrate the thickest part of the flesh and will also help to cook the chicken evenly.

Peel and crush the garlic. Mix the garlic, lemon juice, liquid saffron, olive oil and salt and pepper in a shallow dish large enough to take the birds side by side. Brush the marinade all over the chickens to coat them inside and out. Cover the dish with cling film/plastic wrap and set aside for at least 2 hours. Turn the birds in the marinade a couple of times. You can also prepare the chickens and leave them in the marinade overnight in the fridge.

Cooking

To grill the chickens, you need a very hot barbecue. If it is big enough to allow the two birds to be cooked at the same

Serves 4–6
Preparation: approximately
20–25 minutes, plus marinating
Cooking: 20–30 minutes

Ingredients
2 small whole chickens
1 clove of garlic
125 ml/4 fl oz lemon juice
1 teaspoon liquid saffron (p. 28)
4 tablespoons olive oil
salt and black pepper

time, so much the better. Grill for approximately 10 minutes on each side and baste occasionally with olive oil. Check that they are cooked all the way through to the bone; if not, allow another 5 minutes on each side.

If you are using the oven grill/broiler, preheat it to its highest setting. Put the chicken on a rack in the middle of the oven with an oven tray underneath to catch any marinade and cooking juices. Cook for 10 minutes on each side, or until cooked all the way through, basting occasionally with olive oil.

Serve hot off the grill with plain rice (*chelo*, p. 134) and Cucumber, tomato and onion salad (*Salad-e Shirazi*, p. 181) or mixed herbs (*Sabzi khordan*, p. 17). You can also grill a couple of beef tomatoes (cut in half) to accompany the chicken.

TIP: Use two flat skewers to pierce through the thigh and the breast on either side of the chickens, to make it easier to move the birds on the grill and turn them over.

Right: Preparing Kabab on a picnic.

Meatballs stuffed with prunes in pomegranate syrup
Koofteh aloo

The sweet and sour taste of this dish goes very well with the fresh flavours of Herb rice (*Sabzi polo*, p. 159).

Preparation
Peel and grate the large onion. Peel and chop the small onion.

Wash the herbs in cold water and dry them. Using a sharp, wide-bladed knife, finely chop the fresh green leaves and tender stalks.

Mix the minced/ground meat with the grated onion, chopped herbs, turmeric, salt and pepper. Knead until thoroughly mixed. Divide the mixture into eight equal parts.

Taking one part of the meat mixture, push a prune into the middle and wrap the meat around it to form a ball. Lightly dust with flour and set aside. Repeat until you have eight meatballs.

Cooking
Heat the oil in a large frying pan/skillet and lightly fry the meatballs until golden on all sides. Set aside on kitchen paper.

Add the chopped onion to the oil remaining in the pan and fry until light brown. Stir in the remaining prunes. Return the meatballs to the pan. Reduce the heat. Add the stock, pomegranate syrup and sugar. Simmer gently for about 30 minutes until the sauce is very dark and thickened.

Arrange the meatballs in a shallow serving bowl and pour the sauce around them.

Serves 4
Preparation: approximately 30 minutes
Cooking: approximately 45 minutes

Ingredients

1 large onion
1 small onion
30 g/1 oz fresh parsley
20 g/¾ oz fresh tarragon
400 g/14 oz minced/ground beef (or lamb)
1 teaspoon turmeric
salt and black pepper
16 pitted prunes
1 tablespoon plain/all-purpose flour
2 tablespoons vegetable oil
100 ml/3½ fl oz vegetable/chicken stock
100 ml/3½ fl oz pomegranate syrup (p. 24)
2 tablespoons sugar

Serves 4–6
Preparation: approximately
20 minutes
Cooking: approximately
15 minutes

Ingredients

1 medium onion

400 g/14 oz minced/ground lean beef (or lamb)

2 teaspoons turmeric

salt and black pepper

2 tablespoons plain/all-purpose flour

100 ml/3½ fl oz vegetable oil

TIP: Some *aashes* (thick, hearty soups) combined with *Koofteh ghelgheli* can be served as a main meal. Herb and pomegranate soup (*Aash-e anar*, p. 41) is traditionally served in *ghelgheli*. Or try these meatballs with Barley and herb soup (*Aash-e jo*, p. 43).

Miniature meatballs

Koofteh ghelgheli

The name of this dish literally means 'meatballs that roll', comparing them to marbles. *Koofteh ghelgheli* is quick and easy to prepare and goes particularly well with Sticky rice with yellow beans and dill (*Dampokhtak-e baghala*, p. 144); serve cucumber and yogurt (*Maast va khiar*, p. 187) as a side dish. The meatballs also go well with Rice with green lentils, raisins and dates (*Adas polo*, p. 136), Sour cherry rice (*Albaloo polo*, p. 139) or Rice with cabbage and fresh herbs (*Kalam polo*, p. 149).

Preparation

Peel and grate the onion. Squeeze and discard as much of the juice as possible.

Put the meat in a bowl with the onion, turmeric and salt and pepper and mix thoroughly. Sprinkle the flour over a chopping board. Take a teaspoonful of the meat mixture and roll into a marble-sized ball on the palm of your hand. Roll in the flour and set aside. Repeat until you have used all the meat mixture.

Cooking

In a large frying pan/skillet, heat the oil and fry the meatballs on all sides by gently shaking the pan. This should take only a few minutes.

When you have fried all of them, if you intend to serve with rice, pile them on top of the rice while it is steaming, about 10 minutes before serving the rice. To serve, mix the rice with the meatballs on the serving dish.

You can also add the meatballs to an *aash* and simmer gently for 10 minutes before serving.

Dill and broad bean meatballs
Koofteh shebet baghala

This *koofteh* is very popular in northern Iran. It is very
nutritious and this version has a fresh herby taste. Frozen broad
beans/fava beans, readily available in supermarkets, are fine for
this recipe.

Preparation

Wash the rice in several changes of cold water. Put it in a bowl
with cold salted water to cover and let it soak for about 1 hour.

Blanch the frozen beans in boiling salted water for 1 minute,
drain in a colander and cool under the cold tap. To peel them,
pinch off the skin at one end and squeeze the bean out. Cut
each bean in half lengthwise: you will end up with four slivers
of bright green beans. If you use baby broad beans there is no
need to cut them lengthwise.

Wash and dry the dill and parsley. Cut off the tougher stalks
and discard. Coarsely chop the leaves and tender stalks with a
sharp, wide-bladed knife.

Peel and grate one of the onions. Squeeze and discard as much
of the juice as possible, then put the onion into a bowl. Peel and
slice the remaining two onions.

Cooking

Drain the rice and put it into a saucepan with 400 ml/14 fl oz of
cold water and ½ teaspoon of salt. Cook on a medium heat for
10–15 minutes, until partially cooked: test a few grains to check
that they are al dente. Drain in a colander and leave to cool.

Serves 4–6
Preparation: approximately
30 minutes, plus soaking
Cooking: approximately 1 hour

Ingredients

100 g/3½ oz long-grain rice
200 g/7 oz frozen broad beans/
fava beans
50 g/2 oz fresh dill
30 g/1 oz fresh parsley
3 medium onions
400 g/14 oz minced/ground lean
beef (or lamb)
1 medium egg
2 teaspoons turmeric
salt and black pepper
3 tablespoons vegetable oil
80 g/3 oz butter
1 litre/1¾ pints chicken stock
juice of 1 lemon

In a bowl mix the minced/ground meat, grated onion, dill, parsley, broad beans, 1 teaspoon of turmeric, egg, cooked rice and salt and pepper: the ingredients should be evenly spread through the mixture. Take 2 heaped teaspoons of the meat mixture and roll in the palm of your hand to form a ball slightly large than a golf ball. Repeat until you have 15 to 18 meatballs. Set aside.

Take a heavy-based saucepan large enough to hold all the meatballs in one layer (about 30 cm/12 inches in diameter), and place the pan on a medium heat. Add the oil and butter and heat until foaming. Add the sliced onions and fry until golden. Add the rest of the turmeric and stir. Pour in the stock and the lemon juice, taste and adjust the seasoning and bring to the boil. Gently drop the meatballs into the boiling stock, one at a time. The stock should just cover the meatballs. Reduce the heat and simmer gently for 45 minutes. The stock should reduce and thicken and come halfway up the meatballs in the pan.

TIP: Dropping the meatballs into boiling stock helps them keep their shape and stops them from disintegrating.

Serve with boiled potatoes or fresh flat bread and a salad of tomatoes, red onions and cucumber slices in a lemon juice dressing. In Iran it is traditional to serve pickles such as mango, aubergine/eggplant or garlic with this dish.

Tarragon meatballs
Koofteh tarkhoon

Tarragon is a wonderfully aromatic herb that goes well with the minced/ground meat and tomatoes in this recipe.

Preparation
Wash the rice and cook as for *kateh* (p. 130) or use the same amount of cooked rice.

Peel and grate one of the onions. Squeeze and discard as much of the juice as possible. Peel and slice the remaining onions.

Wash the herbs and dry them in a salad spinner. Discard the tough stalks and any wilting and yellowing leaves. Roughly chop the fresh green leaves.

Wash and dry the chillies but leave them whole.

Put the meat in a bowl, add the grated onion, egg, chopped herbs, 1 teaspoon of turmeric, the cooked rice and salt and pepper. Mix thoroughly. Take 2 heaped teaspoons of the meat mixture and roll in the palm of your hand to form a ball. Repeat until you have 15 to 18 meatballs. Set aside.

Cooking
Take a heavy-based saucepan large enough to hold all the meatballs in one layer (about 30 cm/12 inches in diameter), and place the pan on a medium heat. Add the oil and butter and, when hot, add the sliced onions and fry until golden. Add the remaining turmeric and stir thoroughly. Add the chopped tomatoes, chillies and the stock and bring to the boil. Taste and adjust the seasoning.

Serves 4–6
Preparation: 30–40 minutes,
plus cooking the rice
Cooking: approximately 1 hour

Ingredients
100 g/3½ oz long-grain rice
4 medium onions
20 g/¾ oz fresh tarragon
15 g/½ oz fresh parsley
2–3 green or red chillies
400 g/14 oz minced/ground beef
(or lamb)
1 medium egg
2 teaspoons turmeric
salt and black pepper
3 tablespoons vegetable oil
80 g/3 oz butter
400 g/14 oz canned chopped
tomatoes
1 litre/1¾ pints chicken stock
1 tablespoon liquid saffron
(p. 28)

Gently drop the meatballs into the boiling stock. You should end up with a layer of meatballs, just covered by the tomato and stock mixture. Top up with boiling water if necessary. Reduce the heat and simmer gently for 45 minutes. Taste the sauce after 30 minutes and remove the chillies if you find it too spicy. Add the saffron and let it simmer for another 10 minutes.

Carefully spoon the meatballs into a large shallow bowl. Serve with fresh flat bread or boiled potatoes and a green salad. Sliced fresh onions, radishes and herbs go well with this dish.

Below: Koofteh tarkhoon. Aromatic tarragon gives these spicy meatballs a unique taste.

Potato and beef rissoles

Kotlet sibzamini

This is a favourite childhood comfort food in Iran.

Preparation

Peel and finely chop the onion. Wash the herbs and dry them in a salad spinner. Discard any tough stalks and chop the leaves with a sharp, wide-bladed knife, reserving a few sprigs to garnish the dish.

Cooking

Heat 3 tablespoons of oil in a heavy-based frying pan/skillet and fry the onion until golden. Add the minced/ground meat, turmeric and lime powder. Mix thoroughly and fry for 5–10 minutes, stirring frequently, to brown the meat lightly. Add the chopped herbs, tomato purée/tomato paste and lemon juice. Mix and fry for another 5 minutes on a medium heat; season to taste. Set aside to cool.

Meanwhile, wash the potatoes and boil in their skins until tender. Peel the potatoes and mash them until smooth, adding salt and pepper to taste. Set aside until they are cool enough to handle.

Take a heaped tablespoon of mashed potato. Shape it into a ball. Stick your thumb halfway through the ball to make a hole. Stuff 2 teaspoons of the meat mixture into the hole and cover with the mash. Pat it down to make a round patty approximately 8 cm/3 inches in diameter and about 2 cm/¾ inch thick. You should end up with 8 to 10 patties.

Sprinkle the flour over a clean work surface and cover the patties on all sides with a light dusting of flour.

Serves 4–6
Preparation: 20 minutes, plus cooling
Cooking: approximately 45 minutes

Ingredients

1 medium onion
20 g/¾ oz fresh parsley
30 g/1 oz fresh coriander/cilantro
vegetable oil for frying
250 g/9 oz lean minced/ground beef
2 teaspoons turmeric
1 teaspoon powdered dried lime (p. 21)
1 teaspoon tomato purée/tomato paste
juice of ½ lemon
salt and black pepper
1 kg/2¼ lb medium potatoes
2 tablespoons plain/all-purpose flour

TIP: The tricky part of this recipe is the frying. Use a non-stick pan and make sure the oil is hot and the patties are well coated in flour. Use a spatula as big as the patties for ease of manoeuvring.

Below: You can also serve Kotlet sibzamini with Salad-e anar (p. 173).

Heat a couple of tablespoons of oil in a frying pan/skillet (preferably non-stick) and gently lower the patties into the hot oil. You may have to cook them in batches, depending on the size of your frying pan/skillet. Fry for 5–6 minutes; do not move them too much or they will disintegrate. Use a spatula to turn them over and fry for another 5 minutes, until golden brown. Remove from the pan and drain on kitchen paper.

Arrange the patties on a flat serving dish and garnish with sprigs of fresh herbs. Serve with a tomato and red onion salad, a green salad and/or cucumber and yogurt (*Maast va khiar*, p. 187).

Beef rissoles

Kotlet

These can be eaten hot or cold, as a main dish with fries or in pitta bread with slices of fresh tomatoes and fresh herbs. *Kotlet* goes well with any of the yogurt side dishes (see Chapter 6) and with Cucumber, tomato and onion salad (*Salad-e Shirazi*, p. 181) and all types of pickles. The rissoles are delicious cold and can be made the day before you want to eat them.

In Iran minced/ground lamb is usually used, but this recipe uses lean beef as it's less fatty.

Preparation

Wash and peel the potatoes. Boil them in salted water until just tender. Drain and leave to cool. When cool enough to handle, grate them into a bowl and set aside.

Peel and grate the onion. Squeeze and discard as much of the juice as possible.

Wash and dry the herbs. Top and tail the chives and separate the leaves of the coriander/cilantro and parsley and discard the tough stalks. Finely chop the herbs with a sharp, wide-bladed knife.

Put the meat, grated onion, grated potato, herbs and 2 teaspoons of turmeric in a large deep bowl. Add the egg, salt and pepper and mix. Knead for at least 10 minutes, until all the ingredients are thoroughly mixed.

Sprinkle the flour mixed with turmeric over a large chopping board. Take a golf ball-sized piece of the meat mixture and roll it in the flour mixture. Pat it flat with a spatula and shape it into a triangle, pointed at one end and rounded at the other,

Serves 6–8
Preparation: approximately 1 hour
Cooking: approximately 30 minutes

Ingredients
700 g/1½ lb potatoes
1 large onion
30 g/1 oz fresh herbs (coriander/cilantro, parsley, chives, mixed or singly)
350 g/12 oz lean minced/ground beef
2 teaspoons turmeric
1 large egg
salt and black pepper
4 tablespoons plain/all-purpose flour mixed with 1 tablespoon turmeric
vegetable oil for frying

approximately 1 cm/ ½ inch thick. Make sure the patty is evenly coated in the flour and turmeric mixture. Repeat until you have made 10 to 12 patties.

Above left and right: How to shape kotlets using the palms of your hands.

Cooking

Line a flat dish with kitchen paper and set aside. Heat 2 tablespoons of oil in a large frying pan/skillet. When the oil is sizzling hot, carefully slide the beef patties one by one into the frying pan; you will need to cook them in batches. Do not move the *kotlets* around the pan or they may break. After about 5 minutes, use a spatula to lift a corner to see if the underside is golden brown. Once it is you can turn them over. When both sides are golden brown, remove from the pan and drain on the kitchen paper. Continue until all the patties are fried.

It can be served with a variety of side dishes like *Maast va karafs* (p. 184) or *Maast va khiar* (p. 187).

TIP: The oil needs to be very hot before you start frying the *kotlets*. Allow enough space for each *kotlet* in the frying pan so you can turn it over without damaging the others.

OPPOSITE
Kotlets served with fresh mint and red onions.

Stuffed vegetables

Dolmeh

Stuffed vegetables can be served either as a main course or a first course. The most popular *dolmeh* in Iran is the vine leaf, which is usually stuffed with a mixture of minced meat, rice and herbs and cooked in a sweet and sour sauce. However, many other vegetables are also used for *dolmeh*, including peppers/capsicum, aubergine/eggplant, courgette/zucchini and cabbage leaves. This recipe uses a vegetarian stuffing.

Preparation of stuffing

Wash the split peas, put them in a bowl, pour boiling water over them and soak for 1–2 hours (or follow the instructions on the packet). Alternatively, soak the split peas in cold water overnight. Drain and put the split peas in a saucepan, add 300 ml/10 fl oz of cold water and simmer until al dente (approximately 25–30 minutes). Drain and set aside.

Wash the rice and cook in 300 ml/10 fl oz of boiling water with ½ teaspoon of salt. When the rice is cooked (approximately 10 minutes), drain and set aside to cool. Measure 200 g/7 oz of the cooked rice for this recipe.

Wash and drain the raisins. Soak them in half of the lemon juice for 20 minutes.

Peppers/capsicum

Wash the peppers and dry them. Slice the tops off neatly and set aside; the tops will be used later. Take out the seeds without damaging the sides. Do the same with the beef tomatoes, scooping out the seeds and pulp with a small spoon.

Blanch the peppers, including the tops, by dropping them into a

Serves 4–6
Preparation: approximately
1 hour, plus soaking and cooking
the split peas and rice
Cooking: 45 minutes–1 hour

Ingredients
200 g/7 oz split peas
200 g/7 oz rice
50 g/2 oz raisins
100 ml/3½ fl oz lemon juice
(the juice of 2 lemons)
4 peppers/capsicum of
different colours
2 beef tomatoes
50 g/2 oz walnuts
50 g/2 oz mixed fresh herbs
(equal amounts of parsley,
tarragon, coriander/cilantro,
chives)
30 g/1 oz butter
1 teaspoon tomato purée/
tomato paste
salt and black pepper

OPPOSITE

Capsicum, aubergine and tomato
stuffed with a herb and nut mixture
and cooked in a rich tomato sauce.

saucepan of boiling water for a couple of minutes, until just soft. Drain and cool them under running cold water, or plunge them into a bowl of cold water, taking care not to break them. Drain well.

Chop the walnuts. Wash the herbs and dry them in a salad spinner. Discard the tough stalks and chop the leaves finely using a sharp, wide-bladed knife.

To make the stuffing, mix the cooked split peas and rice, raisins (with the lemon juice), walnuts and chopped herbs. Season well to taste.

Cooking

Preheat the oven to 200°C/400°F/gas mark 6. Butter a shallow ovenproof dish just large enough to hold all the peppers and tomatoes.

Spoon the stuffing into the peppers and tomatoes, filling them to the top and taking care not to damage the sides. Replace the tops of the vegetables. Arrange the stuffed peppers and tomatoes upright in the buttered dish.

Mix the tomato purée/tomato paste with the rest of the lemon juice and salt and pepper and pour evenly over the vegetables. Cook in the preheated oven for 45 minutes to 1 hour. Serve hot or cold.

Aubergines/eggplants

For stuffed aubergines/eggplants, you will need to use small, plump, rounded aubergines. Cut off the stem and use a small sharp knife and a spoon to remove the flesh, taking care not to damage the sides; there should be 1 cm/½ inch of flesh all around. Blanch the aubergines by dropping them into a pan of boiling water for a couple of minutes and then plunging

VARIATIONS

Do the same for courgettes/ zucchini as for aubergines/ eggplants

them into a bowl of ice-cold water. Turn them upside down to drain, and pat dry on kitchen paper. Stuff and cook them as for the peppers.

Stuffed cabbages

For stuffed cabbage leaves, carefully remove eight to ten large cabbage leaves in one piece. Wash the leaves and blanch in boiling water for about 2 minutes. Drain well and leave to cool. Take 1 tablespoon of the stuffing mixture and place it in the middle of a leaf. Fold the sides over the stuffing and roll up to make a parcel.

Melt 30 g/1 oz of butter in a saucepan on a medium heat. Arrange the stuffed leaves in one layer in the pan. Mix 100 ml/ 3½ fl oz of lemon juice, 2 tablespoons of sugar and 1 tablespoon of liquid saffron (p. 28) and pour over the leaves. Cook on a low heat for about 30 minutes.

To serve, remove the parcels carefully to ensure that they remain whole. Serve in a shallow dish and garnish with fresh herbs. Stuffed cabbage leaves are best served hot.

Above: Stuffed cabbage leaves.

Serves 4–6
Preparation: 25 minutes
Cooking: 35–40 minutes

Ingredients
100 g/3½ oz chives (or the
green ends of spring onions/
scallions)
100 g/3½ oz parsley
50 g/2 oz fresh dill
50 g/2 oz fresh coriander/
cilantro
30 g/1 oz fresh mint, oregano (or
any other aromatic herb)
30 g/1 oz walnuts
6 eggs
salt and black pepper
2 tablespoons liquid saffron
(p. 28)
20 g/¾ oz *zereshk* (barberry)
(p. 14)
1 teaspoon turmeric
1 tablespoon plain/all-purpose
flour
1 teaspoon bicarbonate of soda/
baking soda
30 g/1 oz butter
1 tablespoon vegetable oil

Herb omelette
Kookoo

Kookoo is a combination of egg with different herbs and
vegetables such as aubergine/eggplant or potato. The egg is
beaten and used to hold the ingredients together, but it is not
the dominant ingredient. *Kookoo sabzi*, which includes a mixture
of chopped herbs and finely chopped green vegetables, is the
most popular type of *kookoo* in Iran; it can be served hot or cold,
as a first course or a main course.

Kookoo goes well with most yogurt side dishes, such as cucumber
and yogurt (*Maast va khiar*, p. 187) or celery and yogurt (*Maast
va karafs*, p. 184). It is also delicious with Cucumber, tomato and
onion salad (*Salad-e Shirazi*, p. 181) and pickles.

Preparation
Wash the chives, or the green ends of spring onions, keeping
them in a bundle. Cut the chives (or the spring onion ends)
into 2–3 mm/ 1/8 inch lengths and set aside. Wash the parsley,
dill, coriander and other aromatic herbs in cold water and dry
them in a salad spinner or with a clean tea towel. Discard any
tough stalks and yellowing or wilting leaves. Chop the leaves
and tender stalks finely using a sharp, wide-bladed knife. Mix
thoroughly with the chives.

Chop the walnuts. Beat the eggs, season and add the liquid
saffron, stir and set aside.

Cooking
In a large bowl mix the chopped herbs with the *zereshk*,
chopped walnuts, turmeric, flour and bicarbonate of soda. Stir
in the beaten eggs and mix thoroughly.

Melt the butter with the oil in a large, non-stick frying pan/skillet. When hot, add the herb and egg mixture and use a wooden spatula to spread the mixture evenly in the pan. Cover the pan with a lid, reduce the heat and cook on a low heat for approximately 35–40 minutes. The *kookoo* will rise like a cake.

To serve, flip the *kookoo* over into a flat dish, so that the fried side is up.

Below: Intricate brickwork of the interior of a dome.

Chapter 5

RICE

Chapter 5

Rice

OPPOSITE

The patterns and colours in Persian culture resonate from the mosaics in the mosques to the decorative rices of the dinner table.

Rice is an integral element of Persian cuisine and it would be unthinkable to have a large party or reception without various colourful rice dishes, arranged on trays in peaked mounds. Plain, fluffy white rice is called *chelo* in Persian and rice mixed with other ingredients is *polo*. If *chelo* is the king of Persian rice, majestic and aloof, then *polo* is the queen – beautiful, subtle and adorned with a range of ingredients.

The texture of rice depends on the way it is cooked. It can vary from sophisticated, fluffy, separate grains to delicious sticky clumps. It is important to choose the right method to achieve the result you want, and careful attention should be paid to the cooking and presentation of rice dishes.

Of the numerous varieties of rice available, the one most suitable for our purposes is the fragrant basmati, which is the nearest to the famous Persian rice called *dom siah* (black tail).

Styles of rice dishes

• *Chelo* is an aromatic, fluffy, individually grained dish made with top-grade rice and eaten only in conjunction with *khoresht* (Chapter 3) – the sole exception being *Chelo kabab* (p. 103). Served at formal occasions and parties as well as at special family meals, a good *chelo* is invariably accompanied by its *tahdig* crust (p. 131).

• *Polo* is rice in its most varied form, mixed with an array of herbs, pulses, vegetables, fruit or nuts. Different *polos* may include meats, chicken, fish or prawns/shrimp. At formal occasions and parties, a selection of colourful *polos* adds elegance to any dining table. *Polo* is made with top-grade rice and follows the same initial process as *chelo* before the other ingredients are added. Like *chelo*, it will generate a *tahdig* crust (p. 131). Because of the various additional ingredients, a *polo* can be eaten as a stand-alone dish. For simple meals, a *polo* may be the single main course, accompanied by a salad, yogurt or *doogh*, a yogurt-based drink (p. 193).

• *Kateh* is a more informal rice dish, which can be plain (like *chelo*) or mixed with other ingredients (like *polo*). Easier to make than either, it lacks the elegant fluffiness of *chelo* but has its own original aroma, flavours and texture. Plain *kateh* is served with everyday family meals in combination with a *khoresht*. Cooked with herbs and pulses, *kateh* can be served as a meal on its own, like a *polo*.

• *Dampokhtak*, or *dami*, is a variation on *kateh*. The rice is cooked together with pulses and the result is a nutritious sticky rice ideal for cold winter days and stay-at-home evenings.

Standard preparation and cooking methods

The general rule is to wash and soak the rice, then drain and boil it, using one of the methods described below. You then prepare the crusty *tahdig* base and, lastly, steam the rice.

Use a wide, heavy-based saucepan, ideally enamelled cast-iron, which retains heat well and allows slow, even cooking and helps prevent the bottom from burning. Make sure that the pan you use is large enough to allow the rice plenty of space while steaming.

Allow 150 g/5 oz of rice per person as an accompaniment to *khoresht*. You can use more if you are serving the rice on its own as a *polo* (the recipes in this chapter give exact amounts).

Preparation and soaking

Place the rice in a large bowl and add enough cold water to come about 2.5 cm/1 inch above the rice. Gently move the grains around the bowl, using your hands. Drain the water and repeat the rinsing action at least three times or until the water remains reasonably clear. Drain and add cold water to cover the rice by 2.5 cm/1 inch, as before. Add 1 tablespoon of salt per 200 g/7 oz of rice and leave to soak, ideally for at least 2 hours, before cooking.

Cooking *chelo* and *polo* (traditional method)

Drain the soaked rice. Fill a saucepan three-quarters full with cold water. Add 1 tablespoon of salt per 300 g/11 oz of rice. Bring to the boil on a high heat. Add the rice to the boiling water. To begin with, you will see individual grains of rice rising to the surface as the water boils. Gradually, more grains come up to the surface with each bubble. After about 10 minutes, you will see the pattern of bubbles change to waves of rice rising to the top. Count approximately five waves and then remove from the heat. Drain in a fine-meshed colander or a large sieve. Taste a couple of grains. If the rice is too salty, rinse once with cold water.

The rice is now ready for steaming. At this stage you can add other ingredients if you are making a *polo*. Return the empty saucepan to the heat and add vegetable oil (or oil and butter; follow the recipe). Add your chosen *tahdig* ingredient (p. 131). Reduce the heat and gently pile the rice on the *tahdig*, using a slotted spoon and starting from the middle of the pan. Ideally, you will end up with a pyramid of rice that comes short of touching the lid. This will allow the steam to escape from the sides as well as the top, leaving your rice grains separate and fluffy. Drizzle vegetable oil – or oil and butter cut into small pieces – over the top. Wrap the lid in a clean tea towel and put it firmly on the pan to prevent steam from escaping as much as possible. The cloth also absorbs the condensed steam on the lid, preventing it from dropping back into the pan and making the rice soggy. Reduce the heat to low, but make sure that steam rises all the way to the top of the pan. If you have a gas hob, reduce the heat to minimum and use a heat diffuser. Leave to steam for 45 minutes to 1 hour (follow the recipe). It is advisable not to remove the lid during steaming; the crust will form nicely and the rice will not burn. The lid should be hot to the touch and the tea towel should be moist with the steam.

Cooking *kateh*

This is the quick and easy way of cooking rice and the result can be similar if not quite as good as the traditional method.

Measure the rice by volume and soak as described above.

Add an equal volume of cold water (for example, one cup of rice to one cup of water) and pour into a saucepan. Bring to the boil. Drain the soaked rice and add to the boiling water. Add 1 tablespoon of salt per 300 g/11 oz of rice and bring to the boil. Add vegetable oil (or oil and butter; follow the recipe) and cook, uncovered, on a medium heat. Simmer gently without stirring until all the water has been absorbed and small, crater-like holes start to appear on the surface of the rice (approximately 5–10 minutes). Carefully empty the rice into a bowl.

At this stage you can add other ingredients if you are making a *polo*. Return the pan to the heat and add vegetable oil (or oil and butter; follow the recipe). Add your chosen *tahdig* ingredient (below) and gently pile the partially cooked rice onto the *tahdig*, using a slotted spoon. Reduce the heat to low. Drizzle vegetable oil – or a mixture of oil and butter – over the rice. Wrap the lid in a clean tea towel and put it firmly on the pan. Leave to steam on a low heat for 45 minutes to 1 hour (follow the recipe).

Cooking *dampokhtak*

Measure the rice by volume and soak as described above. Drain the soaked rice, rinse once, and tip into a saucepan. Add one and a half measures of boiling water to one measure of rice. Add the cooked pulse mixture, vegetable oil and 1 tablespoon of salt per 300 g/11 oz of rice and cook on a medium heat until all the water has been absorbed, as for *kateh* (above).

Wrap the lid in a clean tea towel and put it firmly on the pan, reduce the heat to low and leave to steam for 40–45 minutes.

Preparing the *tahdig*

During the steaming process a crust will form in the bottom of the pan. This is called the *tahdig* and is a delicious accompaniment to the rice, much prized by Iranians. You can adjust the thickness and flavour of your *tahdig* by adding various ingredients: see the list below. Before returning the boiled rice to the saucepan, heat a mixture of butter and vegetable oil in the pan (just enough to cover the base of the pan) on a medium heat until sizzling. Then cover the bottom of the pan with a layer of your chosen ingredient. Carefully spoon the rice on top, then steam.

If you are making *tahdig* for a *polo*, add all the polo ingredients of your choice to the rice before beginning the *tahdig* process.

Plain rice: Sprinkle in enough of the boiled rice to cover the bottom of the pan.

Bread: Traditionally the thin Persian bread known as *lavash* forms the best bread-based *tahdig*. You can use any Middle

Eastern flat bread or even pitta bread split in half to produce two thin leaves. Western breads, loaves, baguettes etc are not suitable for *tahdig*.

Potatoes: Peel and slice into 2–3 mm/ 1/8 inch thick slices. Wash in cold water to remove the starch, dry on kitchen paper and place them in the bottom of the pan. Other root vegetables can be used in the same way.

Yogurt: Mix a couple of tablespoons of the boiled rice with a couple of tablespoons of Greek-style yogurt and 1 teaspoon of liquid saffron (p. 28) and spread this on the bottom of the pan.

Egg: Mix a couple of tablespoons of the boiled rice with 1 beaten egg and spread thinly over the bottom of the pan.

Lettuce and cabbage leaves can also be used.

Having covered the bottom of the pan with one of the *tahdig* ingredients, sprinkle the remaining rice over this base. Do this gently rather than pouring in all the rice in one go. This will ensure that the rice remains light and separate and creates an even crust on the bottom.

Serving

Before serving, dip the bottom of the saucepan in cold water or stand it in approximately 5 cm/2 inches of cold water in the sink for 1–2 minutes. This helps to loosen the *tahdig* crust at the bottom of the pan so that it will come away easily.

Using a slotted spoon, spoon the rice onto a serving dish. Fluff the rice as you pile it on to the dish. If you have made a *polo* and layered the rice with another mixture, gently mix the two as you serve.

Remove the *tahdig* in pieces and serve them separately in a shallow dish.

Using a rice cooker

An electric rice cooker is a very useful gadget for making Persian rice dishes. It is especially good for making *Chelo* (p. 134) or *Tahchin* (p. 161). It is very easy to use: you put the rice and water in and it does the rest of the job; the *tahdig* (p. 131) is perfect as the heat is even and controlled throughout the steaming process, so the crust forms at the bottom without burning.

I recommend using rice cookers only for cooking plain rice, the resulting *tahdig* would be crispy plain rice.

There are many varieties of rice cooker available in electrical shops and department stores. The simple traditional Japanese rice cooker, now used in most Persian households, has an outer container with the heat element and the thermostat and a graduated inner bowl with a non-stick surface. The manufacturer's instructions specify the proportion of water to rice and the length of steaming required for particular types of rice. The non-stick surface makes it easy to turn out the rice upside down when serving, with the crust on top.

Serves 4
Preparation: 15 minutes,
plus soaking
Cooking: approximately
1 hour

Ingredients

600 g/1 lb 5 oz basmati rice

5 tablespoons salt

50 g/2 oz butter

3 tablespoons vegetable oil

1 large potato, peeled and thinly
sliced (optional)

2 tablespoons liquid saffron
(p. 28) (optional)

Plain white rice

Chelo

Plain rice is the staple of Persian cuisine and the essential accompaniment to any *khoresht* (Chapter 3). *Chelo kabab* (p. 103), charcoal-grilled skewers of lamb with plain rice, is sometimes referred to as Iran's national dish. This is the traditional method, but you can use the *kateh* method (p. 130) if you prefer. This recipe gives instructions for a potato *tahdig*, but you can choose another *tahdig* (p. 131).

Preparation

Place the rice in a large bowl and add enough cold water to come about 2.5 cm/1 inch above the rice. Gently move the grains around the bowl, using your hands. Drain the water and repeat the action at least three times or until the water remains reasonably clear. Drain and add cold water to cover the rice by 2.5 cm/1 inch. Add 3 tablespoons of salt and leave to soak for at least 2 hours.

Cooking

Drain and rinse the rice; drain again. Fill a heavy-based saucepan (ideally 25 cm/10 inches in diameter) three-quarters full with cold water. Add 2 tablespoons of salt. Bring to the boil on a high heat. Add the drained rice to the boiling water. Do not cover. To begin with, you will see individual grains of rice rising to the surface as the water boils. Gradually, more grains come up to the surface with each bubble. After about 10 minutes, you will see the pattern of bubbles change to waves of rice rising to the surface. Count approximately five waves and then remove from the heat and drain the rice in a colander. Adjust the salt to taste: rinse the rice once if too salty or add a little more salt if necessary.

Return the saucepan to a medium heat. Add 20 g/¾ oz of butter and 2 tablespoons of oil. When sizzling, cover the bottom of the pan with the sliced potato, if using (or choose another *tahdig*, p. 131). Using a slotted spoon, gently pile on the rice, starting from the centre and creating a pyramid. Take care not to break the grains. Drizzle the rest of the butter and oil on top. Wrap the lid in a clean tea towel and place tightly on the pan. Leave to steam on a very low heat (on a gas flame use the lowest setting and a heat diffuser) for 45–50 minutes. When you remove the lid the grains of rice should be thoroughly cooked and fluffy.

When the rice is ready, dip the bottom of the saucepan in the sink filled with 5 cm/2 inches of cold water to loosen the crust. Serve the rice on to a shallow serving dish, fluffing up the rice as you serve. Drizzle the saffron over the rice, if using. Once all the rice is removed the layer of crispy potatoes should easily come away from the bottom of the pan; serve this on a separate plate.

Above: *Chelo is Persian plain rice with fluffy long grains decorated with saffron.*

Serves 4–6
Preparation: 35 minutes,
plus soaking
Cooking: approximately
1½ hours

Ingredients

400 g/14 oz basmati rice

3 tablespoons salt

150 g/5 oz green lentils

100 g/3½ oz raisins (or sultanas/
golden raisins)

50 g/2 oz dates

1 medium onion

2 medium potatoes for the *tahdig*
(p. 131) (optional)

approximately 1 litre/1¾ pints
water

150 g/5 oz butter

100 ml/3½ fl oz vegetable oil

2 teaspoons turmeric

4 tablespoons liquid saffron
(p. 28)

Rice with green lentils, raisins and dates
Adas polo

This is a delicious, nutritious dish that can be served as a vegetarian meal or accompanied by lamb, chicken or Miniature meatballs (p. 108). In Shiraz, in southern Iran, it is traditionally cooked without raisins and dates, especially when accompanied by chicken or meat. However, the combination of green lentils, raisins and dates creates a very good vegetarian dish. It is a useful recipe as the ingredients are available all year round. It is not time-consuming to prepare and cook and the result is very rewarding.

Preparation

Wash the rice and soak for 2 hours (see Preparation and soaking, p. 129).

Wash the lentils thoroughly and drain them. Wash the raisins and pat dry on kitchen paper. Take the stones/pits out of the dates and chop them to the same size as the raisins. Peel the onion and chop it finely.

Wash, peel and thinly slice the potatoes, if using, and put them in a bowl of cold water to prevent discoloration.

Cooking

Put the lentils in a saucepan and add about 500 ml/just under 1 pint of cold water; do not add salt. Bring to the boil and cook on a medium heat until the lentils are al dente. Drain and set aside.

Heat 30 g/1 oz of the butter and 2 tablespoons of oil in a frying pan/skillet on a medium heat and fry the onion until golden.

Reduce the heat and add the raisins and dates and stir. Add the cooked lentils and 1 teaspoon of turmeric. Add salt to taste. Stir and set aside.

Pour 400 ml/14 fl oz of water into a heavy-based saucepan and bring to the boil. Drain the rice and add to the boiling water with 1 tablespoon of salt, 50 g/2 oz of butter and 3 tablespoons of oil. Leave to simmer, uncovered, on a medium heat, until all the water has been absorbed and holes start to appear on the surface of the rice (approximately 10 minutes).

Above: Adas polo is a festive dish of nutty lentils and aromatic rice with sweet raisins and dates.

Tip the rice into a shallow dish. (To make a rice *tahdig* (instead of potato), set aside 2 heaped tablespoons of the plain rice.) Gently fold the lentil and raisin mixture into the rice and add 3 tablespoons of the liquid saffron – take care not to break the grains of rice as you mix.

If you are using potatoes for the *tahdig*, drain and dry the potato slices. Return the saucepan to the heat. Add 2 tablespoons of vegetable oil and when it is sizzling arrange the sliced potatoes in a layer to cover the bottom of the pan. (Alternatively, you can use a couple of tablespoons of cooked plain rice instead of potato slices, or make other types of *tahdig*, p. 131.)

Spoon the lentil and rice mixture over the layer of potatoes. Keep the rice in a pyramid shape and away from the sides of the pan as much as possible. Dot the rest of the butter on top of the rice. Wrap the lid in a clean tea towel and place it firmly on the pan. Leave to steam on a low heat (with a heat diffuser on a gas flame) for 50 minutes to 1 hour.

When the rice is ready, dip the bottom of the pan in cold water, or stand the pan in 5 cm/2 inches of cold water for few minutes, to help release the bottom layer. Serve the rice in a shallow dish, fluffing it as you spoon it out. Drizzle the remaining liquid saffron over the rice. Detach and break the crispy layer of potatoes or plain rice from the bottom of the pan and serve on a separate plate.

To serve, accompany with a dish of fresh herbs, radishes and spring onions/scallions. Mango chutney or pickles also go well with this dish.

TIPS: Lentils absorb a lot of oil, so you might need to add more butter to the rice when serving, if you find the rice to be dry.

Do not use rice mixed with lentils for the *tahdig*: the lentils turn into hard pellets in the oil and the raisins and dates burn.

Sour cherry rice
Albaloo polo

This is an elegant and colourful dish, the dark red of the cherries making an attractive contrast to the yellowy-orange of saffron; you can almost taste the combination of sweet and sour cherries with the perfumed nuttiness of the rice just by looking at it. In Iran, *Albaloo polo* is traditionally made with fresh sour cherries in season, but frozen morello cherries, available from good supermarkets, can also be used. This is an easy rice dish to make. It can be served with Miniature meatballs (p. 108) or Saffron lemon chicken (p. 97).

Preparation
Wash the rice and soak for 2 hours (see Preparation and soaking, p. 129).

Thaw the frozen cherries.

Cooking
Pat the thawed cherries on kitchen paper to blot up the excess liquid. Put the cherries in a saucepan with the sugar and gradually bring to the boil. Let them simmer gently for 15 minutes to reduce the juice. Add the lemon juice and continue to cook for another couple of minutes; you will end up with a thick, but still liquid, compote consistency. Set aside.

Drain the rice. Measure 60 ml/2 fl oz of the juice from the cooked cherries and place in a medium-sized, heavy-based saucepan. Add the water and bring back to the boil. Add the drained rice, 30 g/1 oz of butter and 2 tablespoons of oil. Add salt to taste. Bring back to the boil, reduce the heat and simmer gently, uncovered, until all the water has been absorbed (approximately 10 minutes). You will see holes appear in the surface of the rice.

Serves 4
Preparation: 10 minutes, plus soaking
Cooking: approximately 1½ hours

Ingredients
500 g/1 lb 2 oz basmati rice
2–3 tablespoons salt
500 g/1 lb 2 oz fresh/frozen pitted morello cherries
150 g/5 oz sugar
juice of ½ lemon
400 ml/14 fl oz boiling water
50 g/2 oz butter
3 tablespoons vegetable oil
2 tablespoons liquid saffron (p. 28)
30 g/1 oz pistachios, cut into slivers (optional)

Above: *Albaloo polo is a mouth-watering combination of morello cherries, saffron and basmati rice.*

Tip the rice out into a bowl. Return the pan to the heat and add the rest of the butter and 1 tablespoon of oil. When sizzling, sprinkle a layer of the boiled rice over the bottom of the pan, to make the *tahdig* (p. 131). Now add alternate layers of rice and cherry mixture, piling them up in the centre of the pan, away from the sides as much as possible. Wrap the lid in a clean tea towel and place it firmly on the pan. Leave to steam on a low heat for 45–50 minutes.

When the rice is ready, stand the pan in 5 cm/2 inches of cold water for 1–2 minutes to help the *tahdig* to come away more easily. Serve the rice on a shallow serving dish, fluffing it as you spoon it out. Set aside 1 tablespoon of the rice and cherry mixture in a small bowl; mix with the saffron liquid and scatter over the top. Decorate with pistachio slivers, if using. Break the *tahdig* into small pieces and serve on a separate plate.

The fruity, sweet and sour taste of *Albaloo polo* does not need too many additional flavours. A simple green salad with lemon and olive oil dressing would suffice.

Broad beans and dill rice

Baghala polo

Fresh broad beans/fava beans, dill and rice together create an extraordinary combination with a fresh, herby flavour, which reminds you that spring is here. More often than not, this dish is served with lamb, such as Saffron yogurt lamb (p. 93), although it is equally good with Saffron lemon chicken (p. 97) or Roast chicken (p. 98). The beans require some fiddly preparation, but the result is worth it.

Preparation

Wash the rice and soak for 2 hours (see Preparation and soaking, p. 129).

If you are using frozen beans, pour boiling water over them, then drain immediately and peel off the skin (you do not need to blanch fresh beans). Cut the resulting bright green beans in half lengthwise, separating them into four long pieces. If you are using frozen baby broad beans, just peel them; they will not need to be cut in half. If you like, you can set aside 1 tablespoon of the prepared broad beans for the garnish.

Wash the fresh dill and dry it thoroughly in a salad spinner. Discard the tough stalks and finely chop the feathery leaves. Peel the garlic and chop finely. Mix the fresh or dried dill with the chopped garlic and set aside.

Wash, peel and thinly slice the potatoes, if using, and put them in a bowl of cold water to prevent discoloration.

Cooking

Half-fill a large, heavy-based saucepan with cold water and add 1½ tablespoons of salt. Bring to the boil on a high heat. Drain

Serves 4
Preparation: 1 hour,
plus soaking
Cooking: approximately
1½ hours

Ingredients

300 g/11 oz basmati rice

2 tablespoons salt

500 g/1 lb 2 oz shelled broad beans/fava beans (fresh or frozen) (or approximately 4 kg/ 9 lb broad beans in their pods)

200 g/7 oz fresh dill or 30 g/1 oz dried dill

2 cloves of garlic

2 medium potatoes for the *tahdig* (p. 131) (optional)

2 teaspoons turmeric

150 g/5 oz butter

4 tablespoons vegetable oil

2 tablespoons liquid saffron (p. 28)

Garnish (optional)

30 g/1 oz butter

1 tablespoon vegetable oil

1 clove of garlic, finely chopped

1 teaspoon liquid saffron (p. 28)

the rice and add to the boiling water. Add the broad beans and turmeric and bring back to the boil. Do not cover. Boil until the individual bubbles turn into waves of rice rising to the surface.

Drain the rice and broad beans into a large colander. Return the saucepan to a medium heat. Add 50 g/2 oz of butter and 2 tablespoons of oil and, when sizzling, cover the bottom of the pan with a layer of sliced potatoes. Alternatively, make another type of *tahdig* (p. 131).

Mix the chopped dill and garlic with the rice and broad beans. Take care not to break the grains of rice. Spoon the rice over the layer of potatoes, starting in the centre of the pan and avoiding the sides as much as possible. Drizzle the rest of the butter and oil on top. Wrap the lid in a clean tea towel and place it firmly on the pan. Leave to steam on a low heat (on a gas flame use the lowest setting and a heat diffuser) for 50 minutes to 1 hour. When you remove the lid the grains of rice should be thoroughly cooked and fluffy.

When the rice is ready, dip the bottom of the pan in cold water to loosen the crust. Spoon the rice onto a shallow serving dish, fluffing up the grains as you serve. Drizzle the liquid saffron over the rice. The layer of crispy potatoes should come away from the bottom of the pan easily. This can be served on a separate plate.

Garnish (optional)

Heat the butter and vegetable oil in a small frying pan/skillet and lightly fry the garlic. Remove from the heat. Mix in the reserved 1 tablespoon of broad beans and the liquid saffron. Spread the garnish over the rice.

Serve with fresh herbs, *Sabzi khordan* (p. 17/Chapter 1), which is a staple of the Persian dinner table. Other side dishes could include cucumber, tomato and onion salad (p. 181).

OPPOSITE

The coming together of fresh dill and broad beans with rice in Baghala polo is spring on a plate.

TIPS: When you add the turmeric to the water it turns a strong yellowy-orange colour, but don't worry: the colour pales to just a hint of yellow in the finished dish.

Pickles also go well with *Baghala polo*.

Serves 4
Preparation: 15 minutes,
plus soaking
Cooking: approximately
1½ hours

Ingredients
300 g/11 oz long-grain rice
1½–2 tablespoons salt
200 g/7 oz dried (yellow) broad
beans/fava beans
50 g/2 oz fresh dill (or 15 g/
½ oz dried dill)
2 medium onions
80 g/3 oz butter
5 tablespoons vegetable oil
2 teaspoons turmeric
1 litre/1¾ pints vegetable (or
meat stock)
600 ml/1 pint cold water
black pepper
2 medium potatoes, peeled and
thinly sliced

Sticky rice with yellow beans and dill

Dampokhtak-e baghala

This is an excellent vegetarian dish, made from dried broad beans/fava beans. Instead of fluffy, individual grains, the rice forms sticky clumps with the aroma of turmeric and dill. The broad beans used for this dish are dried, peeled, small, yellow and split into two lobes. Some supermarkets have them and you can always find them in Middle Eastern shops, especially Lebanese ones. This is very easy to cook.

Preparation
Wash the rice and soak for 2 hours (see Preparation and soaking, p. 129). Wash the beans and soak in cold water for 2 hours.

Wash the dill and dry it in a salad spinner or a clean tea towel. Discard the tough stalks and finely chop the feathery leaves. Peel the onions and roughly chop them.

Cooking
Heat the butter and 3 tablespoons of the oil in a medium-sized, heavy-based saucepan. Fry the onions until golden brown: the caramelized aroma of the fried onions enhances the flavour of the beans in the finished dish.

Add the turmeric and stir thoroughly. Drain the beans and add to the pan with the chopped fresh or dried dill. Stir to coat the beans with the onion and turmeric mixture. Add the stock, bring to the boil and simmer, uncovered, for 30 minutes until the beans are almost cooked.

At this stage the liquid in the pan should be about one-third of the original amount. Drain the rice and add to the beans. Add 600 ml/1 pint of cold water and stir thoroughly. Bring to the boil and add salt and pepper to taste. Reduce the heat to medium and cover with the lid.

After 15–20 minutes the liquid in the pan should have been completely absorbed. Empty the rice and beans into a bowl. Return the pan to the heat. Put the remaining 2 tablespoons of oil into the pan. When hot, arrange the sliced potatoes in a layer at the bottom of the pan. Spoon the rice mixture on top of the layer of potatoes. Pile the rice in the centre of the pan, avoiding the sides as much as possible. Wrap the lid in a clean tea towel and place tightly on the pan. Leave to steam on a low heat for 30 minutes.

When the rice is ready, dip the bottom of the pan in cold water. This helps the crispy layer of potatoes to come away from the pan easily. Serve the rice on a platter. Separate the potato slices as much as possible and serve them on a separate plate.

Salad Shirazi (p. 181) or *maast va khiar* (p. 187) go well with *dampokhtak*.

✳

VARIATION

This can be served with Miniature meatballs (p. 108). Place the meatballs on top of the rice 10 minutes before serving, replace the lid and let the flavour of the meatballs penetrate the rice.

Serves 4–6
Preparation: 15 minutes, plus soaking
Cooking: approximately 3½ hours

Ingredients

150 g/5 oz split peas

500 g/1 lb 2 oz basmati rice

1 kg/2¼ lb shoulder of lamb on the bone

2 medium onions

7 tablespoons vegetable oil

1 teaspoon turmeric

2 whole dried limes (p. 21)

salt and black pepper

2 litres/3½ pints boiling water

100 g/3½ oz butter

100 g/3½ oz raisins

2 tablespoons powdered dried lime (p. 21)

1 tablespoon rice spice (*advieh polo*)

2 tablespoons sugar

4 tablespoons liquid saffron (p. 28)

Lamb, split peas and raisins rice
Kaboli polo

This dish originally comes from Afghanistan and has been adopted in Persia with some variations. Some recipes contain dates as well as raisins. The lime powder adds a distinctive aroma and flavour to the rice. *Advieh* is a typically Persian blend of spices available from Middle Eastern stores. Look for a blend made for rice dishes, but if it is not available, you can do without it. Although relatively time-consuming, this is quite a straightforward dish to cook and the end result is nutritious and delicious.

Preparation

Wash the split peas, put them in a bowl, cover with boiling water and soak for 2 hours (or follow the instructions on the packet). Alternatively, soak the split peas in cold water overnight.

Wash the rice and soak for 2 hours (see Preparation and soaking, p. 129).

Wash the meat and trim off the excess fat.

Peel the onions; chop one of them finely and cut the other into four wedges.

Cooking

Heat 2 tablespoons of oil in a medium-sized, heavy-based saucepan and fry the onion wedges for 2–3 minutes. Add the meat and seal it on all sides. Add the turmeric, the whole dried limes, salt and pepper and stir well, add 500 ml/just under 1 pint of boiling water, cover and bring to the boil.

Reduce the heat and simmer gently for approximately 2–2½ hours, until the meat is completely cooked and coming off the bone. Remove the meat from the pan, cut the meat off the bone and set aside to cool. Boil the sauce to reduce to about 250 ml/9 fl oz.

With your fingers, break the cooked meat into smaller chunks and return to the pan, set aside.

While the meat is cooking, drain the split peas and cook them in a small saucepan with 1 litre/1¾ pints of boiling water (do not add salt). This should take approximately 30 minutes; make sure not to overcook the split peas. When they are tender, drain off the excess water and set aside.

In a large frying pan/skillet, heat 2 tablespoons of oil and 30 g/1 oz butter and fry the chopped onion until golden. Add the raisins, stir well and fry for 1–2 minutes, then add the meat, split peas, lime powder, rice spice, sugar and 2 tablespoons of the liquid saffron, stir and fry for a further 2–3 minutes, remove from the heat and cover with a lid to keep warm.

To cook the rice, boil 400 ml/14 fl oz of water in a large saucepan, big enough to accommodate the rice plus the meat and split peas mixture.

Drain the rice and add to the boiling water. Add 1 tablespoon of salt, 2 tablespoons of oil and 30 g/1 oz butter. Bring back to the boil, then reduce the heat and simmer until all the water has been absorbed and holes appear on the surface of the rice.

Tip the rice into a shallow bowl. Put 2 heaped tablespoons of the cooked rice aside for the *tahdig* (p. 131). Fold the meat and split peas mixture into the rice, very gently mixing all the ingredients.

Rinse the pan and return to the heat. Add 1 tablespoon of oil and 20 g/¾ oz of butter and, when sizzling, sprinkle the 2 tablespoons of rice over the bottom of the pan. Spoon the rice and meat mixture into the middle of the pan, forming a pyramid shape and leaving the sides clear as much as possible. Cut the remaining 20 g/¾ oz of butter into small pieces and dot over the rice. Wrap the lid in a clean tea towel and place firmly on the saucepan. Let the rice steam on a low heat for 1 hour.

When the rice is ready, stand the pan in 5cm/2 inches of cold water in the sink for 1–2 minutes to help release the crust at the bottom of the pan.

Serve the rice in a large shallow dish, arranging the chunks of meat in the middle. Drizzle the remaining saffron liquid on the top. Break the *tahdig* into small pieces and serve on a separate plate.

Kaboli polo goes very well with yogurt and cucumber (p. 187) and parsley and tomato salad (p. 175).

Rice with cabbage and fresh herbs

Kalam polo Shirazi

My version of *Kalam polo* comes from Shiraz in the south of Iran. In this version the fresh aromatic herbs dominate the smell of the cabbage. Variations originating from other parts of Iran do not include as many herbs. White cabbage is the best type to use, but this dish can also be made with green cabbage or kohlrabi. You can use any of the *tahdigs* (p. 131) for this dish but traditionally the *tahdig* is made using the outer leaves of the cabbage. This is a good way of using seasonal and easily affordable ingredients to prepare a healthy and delicious meal. *Kalam polo* can accompany lamb or chicken dishes or Miniature meatballs (p. 108).

Preparation

Wash the rice and soak for 2 hours (see Preparation and soaking, p. 129).

Wash the herbs and dry in a salad spinner. Pinch off the fresh young leaves Finely chop all the herbs. Peel and roughly chop the onion.

Remove 4 or 5 of the outer leaves of the cabbage and set aside to use for the *tahdig*. Cut the cabbage into quarters and cut out the central hard stalk together with as many of the hard veins as you can. You should end up with 350 g/12 oz of tender cabbage leaves; shred the leaves into 1 cm/½ inch strips.

If you are using potatoes for the *tahdig*, wash, peel and thinly slice them. Keep them in a bowl of cold water to prevent discoloration.

Serves 4–6
Preparation: 15 minutes,
plus soaking
Cooking: approximately
1½ hours

Ingredients

500 g/1 lb 2 oz basmati rice
3–4 tablespoons salt
100 g/3½ oz fresh parsley
100 g/3½ oz fresh dill
30 g/1 oz fresh basil
30 g/1 oz fresh tarragon
350 g/12 oz white cabbage
2 medium potatoes (or 4–5 large outside leaves of the cabbage) for the *tahdig* (p. 131) (optional)
1 small onion
3 tablespoons vegetable oil
100 g/3½ oz butter
3 teaspoons turmeric
black pepper
450 ml/15 fl oz water

Cooking

In a large frying pan/skillet, heat 2 tablespoons of vegetable oil and 20 g/¾ oz of butter and fry the onion until golden. Add the shredded cabbage, 1 teaspoon of turmeric, salt and pepper and fry until golden brown.

Use a heavy-based saucepan large enough to accommodate all the ingredients. Bring the water to the boil and add 1 teaspoon of turmeric. Drain the rice and add to the pan, with 1 tablespoon of salt. Cook until the water is absorbed and you can see holes appearing on the surface of the rice. Turn the rice out into a large bowl. If you are not using potatoes or cabbage leaves for the *tahdig*, put 2 heaped tablespoons of the cooked rice aside for this purpose.

Mix the chopped herbs and the cabbage with the rice, making sure they are evenly distributed. Return the saucepan to the heat. Add the remaining 1 tablespoon of oil and 20 g/¾ oz of the butter and heat until foaming. Line the bottom of the pan with the cabbage leaves or, if you are using potato slices, arrange them to cover the bottom of the pan; alternatively, sprinkle the pan with the cooked rice you have set aside.

Gently pile the rice and cabbage mixture into the pan, starting in the middle. Try to keep the pile away from the sides as much as possible. Cut the remaining butter into small pieces and dot over the rice. Wrap the lid in a clean tea towel and place it on the pan. Reduce the heat to minimum and let the rice steam for 50 minutes to 1 hour.

When the rice is ready, dip the bottom of the pan in cold water to help loosen the *tahdig*. Serve the rice onto a large shallow platter. Cut the crispy *tahdig* into small portions and arrange on a separate plate.

TIP: Parsley and tomato salad (p. 175) is a suitable accompaniment to this dish.

Green beans and lamb rice

Lubia polo

This is a very filling dish. The meat and beans are cooked in rich tomato sauce and the hint of cinnamon enhances the flavour. It can be made all year round with frozen green beans.

Preparation

Wash the rice and soak for 2 hours (see Preparation and soaking, p. 129).

Wash the lamb and pat dry on kitchen paper. Trim off any skin and fat and cut the meat into 3 cm/1¼ inch cubes.

Wash and top and tail the beans. Cut them into 5 cm/2 inch lengths. Peel and roughly chop the onion. Put the tomato purée/tomato paste into a bowl, add 250 ml/9 fl oz hot water and stir to dissolve.

Wash, peel and thinly slice the potatoes, if using, and put them in a bowl of cold water to prevent discoloration.

Cooking

In a large, heavy-based saucepan heat 3 tablespoons of oil and fry the onion until golden. Add the meat and stir to seal on all sides. Add the cinnamon, turmeric and salt and pepper to taste. Mix thoroughly to coat the meat in the spices. Add the chopped tomatoes and stir in the tomato puree/tomato paste. Reduce the heat to medium, cover with a lid and cook for 1 hour.

When the meat is tender, remove it using a slotted spoon and set aside.

Serves 4
Preparation: 20 minutes,
plus soaking
Cooking: approximately 2 hours

Ingredients

500 g/1 lb 2 oz basmati rice
3 tablespoons salt
400 g/14 oz lean leg of lamb
200 g/7 oz green beans (fresh or frozen)
1 medium onion
100 g/3½ oz tomato purée/ tomato paste
2 medium potatoes for the *tahdig* (p. 131) (optional)
4 tablespoons vegetable oil
1 teaspoon turmeric
2 teaspoons cinnamon
400 g/14 oz canned chopped tomatoes
400 ml/14 fl oz cold water
100 g/3½ oz butter
black pepper

You should have about 100 ml/3½ fl oz of thick sauce left in the pan; add 400 ml/14 fl oz of cold water and bring the liquid to the boil. Drain the rice and add to the pan, together with 50 g/2 oz of butter. Simmer until all the water has been absorbed and holes start to appear in the surface of the rice.

Turn the rice out into a large bowl. To make a rice *tahdig* (instead of potato), set aside 2 heaped tablespoons of the rice. Mix the beans and meat together and fold into the rice; mix gently but thoroughly. Taste and adjust the seasoning.

Return the saucepan to the heat, add the remaining 1 tablespoon of oil and place on a medium heat until sizzling. Cover the bottom of the pan with the cooked rice you have set aside, or a layer of thinly sliced potato. Spoon the rice and meat mixture into the pan, piling the rice in the centre, away from the sides as much as possible. Cut the remaining 50 g/2 oz butter into small pieces and sprinkle over the rice.

Reduce the heat to minimum. Wrap the lid in a clean tea towel and place it tightly on the pan. Let steam for 1 hour.

When the rice is ready, dip the bottom of the pan in cold water to help loosen the crusty bottom layer. Serve the rice onto a shallow platter, fluffing the grains as you serve to avoid clumps. Cut the crispy layer into small pieces and arrange them on a separate plate.

Serve with cucumber and yogurt (p. 187), various pickles and a selection of fresh herbs, or *sabzi khordan* (p. 17/Chapter 1).

Prawns and raisins rice

Maygoo polo

This dish, from Bushehr on the Persian Gulf, is very easy to prepare and cook. The combination of prawns, dried lime powder, raisins and saffron rice is wonderful. This version includes cumin seeds – an additional aroma that goes well with prawns/shrimp.

Preparation

Wash the rice and soak for 2 hours (see Preparation and soaking, p. 129).

Peel and chop the onion.

Cooking

In a large frying pan/skillet, heat 3 tablespoons of the oil and fry the onion until golden. Add the prawns/shrimp, turmeric and the lime powder, stir and fry for 2–3 minutes. Take care not to overcook the prawns as they will be steamed in the rice. Add the raisins and the cumin seeds, salt and pepper to taste, stir well and remove from the heat; cover with a lid to keep warm.

Put the water in a large heavy-based saucepan and bring to the boil. Drain the rice and add to the boiling water with 1 tablespoon of salt. Simmer until the water is absorbed and you can see holes appearing on the surface of the rice.

Turn the rice out into a large bowl. Set aside 2 heaped tablespoons of rice for the *tahdig* (p. 131).

Fold the prawn and raisin mixture into the rice. Rinse and return the saucepan to the heat, add half of the butter and 1 tablespoon of oil. When foaming, sprinkle the 2 tablespoons

Serves 4
Preparation: 15 minutes,
plus soaking
Cooking: approximately
1 ¼ hours

Ingredients
600 g/1 lb 5 oz rice
3½ tablespoons salt
1 large onion
4 tablespoons vegetable oil
500 g/1 lb 2 oz cooked peeled large prawns/shrimp
1 teaspoon turmeric
2 teaspoons powdered dried lime (p. 21)
100 g/3½ oz raisins
2 teaspoons cumin seeds
salt and black pepper
500 ml/just under 1 pint water
50 g/2 oz butter
2 tablespoons liquid saffron (p. 28)

of plain cooked rice over the bottom of the pan, and then pile up the rice and prawn mixture in the middle of the pan.

Cut the remaining butter into small pieces and dot over the rice. Wrap the lid in a clean tea towel and place it tightly on the pan. Reduce the heat to minimum and let the rice steam for 50 minutes to 1 hour.

When the rice is ready, stand the pan in 5 cm/2 inches of cold water in the sink to help loosen the *tahdig*. Serve the rice onto a large shallow serving dish and pour the liquid saffron over the top. Cut the *tahdig* into small pieces and serve on a plate.

This dish goes well with chicory and orange salad (p. 177) and carrot and cumin salad (p. 176).

※

Saffron jewelled rice
Morassa' polo

Also known as *Shirin polo*, *Morassa' polo* is a very colourful and fragrant dish. It is traditionally served with Lamb and split peas (*Khoresht-e gheimeh*, p. 77), but works equally well with Saffron lemon chicken (*Joojeh za'farani*, p. 97). Some versions use slivers of carrot and even barberries (*zereshk*) for extra colour and to create an intriguing sweet-and-sour taste. The aroma of saffron should be dominant in this rice; feel free to add more saffron if you like. *Morassa' polo* is not difficult to make, but attention to detail is needed if you are seeking a perfect result for a special occasion.

Preparation
Wash the rice and soak with 2 tablespoons of salt for 2 hours (see Preparation and soaking, p. 129).

Using a small sharp knife or a vegetable peeler, peel the oranges, avoiding the white pith and trimming away as much pith as possible. Cut the peel into uniform matchsticks (juliennes). To reduce the bitterness of the orange peel, bring a small saucepan of water to the boil, drop in the orange peel juliennes and bring back to the boil. Remove from the heat and drain in a sieve. Taste the peel and repeat the blanching if necessary. Drain the peel and set aside.

Cooking
Put 125 ml/4 fl oz of water, the sugar and 3 tablespoons of liquid saffron in a small saucepan. Put on a low heat and let the sugar dissolve.

Add the pistachios, almonds and blanched orange peel. Mix thoroughly and bring to the boil. As soon as the mixture starts

Serves 4–6
Preparation: 25 minutes,
plus soaking
Cooking: approximately
1¼ hours

Ingredients
600 g/1 lb 5 oz basmati rice
3 tablespoons salt
1 or 2 oranges (preferably unwaxed)
approximately 750 ml/ 1¼ pints water
250 g/9 oz sugar
100 ml/3½ fl oz liquid saffron (p. 28)
50 g/2 oz pistachio slivers
50 g/2 oz almond slivers
6 tablespoons vegetable oil
50 g/2 oz butter

PREVIOUS PAGE

Morassa' polo is a festive dish with the aroma of saffron and orange zest and the crunchiness of almonds and pistachios.

bubbling remove from the heat and set aside. The mixture should have the consistency of a thick syrup and have the colour and scent of saffron. Add more liquid saffron if needed.

Pour 2 tablespoons of liquid saffron and 3 tablespoons of oil in a small pan, bring to the boil and set aside.

Put 550 ml/just under 1 pint water in a large, heavy-based saucepan and bring to the boil. Add 2 tablespoons of liquid saffron and 1 tablespoon of salt. Drain the rice and add to the pan. Bring back to the boil and then simmer until all the water has been absorbed and holes appear on the surface of the rice.

Tip the rice into a shallow bowl. Set aside 2 tablespoons of plain rice for the *tahdig*. Set aside 1 tablespoon of the nut and peel mixture for the garnish. Mix the rest of the nut and peel mixture thoroughly with the rice.

Return the pan to the heat. Put the remaining 3 tablespoons of oil into the pan on a medium heat until sizzling. Sprinkle the rice you have set aside for the *tahdig* over the bottom of the pan. Using a slotted spoon, spoon the rice and nut mixture into the middle of the pan, avoiding the sides as much as possible. Cut the butter into small pieces and dot over the rice. Wrap the lid in a clean tea towel and place firmly on the pan. Reduce the heat to minimum (on a gas flame use the lowest setting and a heat diffuser) and steam for 45–50 minutes.

When the rice is ready, stand the pan in 5 cm/2 inches of cold water for 1–2 minutes to loosen the crispy *tahdig*. Serve the rice onto a shallow dish, fluffing the grains. Pour the reserved nut and peel mixture on top as garnish. Drizzle the oil and saffron mixture over the garnished rice. Remove the crispy layer from the pan, cut into small pieces and serve on a separate plate.

Herb rice
Sabzi polo

For the Persian New Year (Norouz) celebrations it is traditional to serve this rice dish with fish – traditionally fillets of smoked white fish from the Caspian Sea. However, fresh fish is now widely available. In the north of Iran it is marinated in lemon juice and saffron and fried, while in the south the fish is stuffed and baked. This rice goes well with most fish and meat dishes.

Preparation
Wash the rice and soak for 2 hours (see Preparation and soaking, p. 129).

Wash the parsley, dill and coriander/cilantro and discard the tough stalks and any yellowing or wilting leaves. Pinch off the leaves and tender stalks and wash in cold water, then dry in a salad spinner or with a clean tea towel. Chop the herbs finely using a sharp, wide-bladed knife. Wash the chives, keeping them in a bundle. Cut the chives in 2–3 mm/ 1/8 inch lengths. Mix the chives with the rest of the herbs.

Peel the garlic and chop finely. If you are using fresh green garlic chop it and mix with the rest of the herbs.

Wash and peel the potatoes and slice them thinly. Put them in a bowl of cold water to prevent discoloration.

Cooking
Half-fill a large, heavy-based saucepan with water and 2 tablespoons of salt. Bring to the boil. Drain the rice and add to the boiling water, together with the turmeric. Boil, uncovered, until the individual bubbles turn into waves of rice rising to the surface. Drain the rice in a colander. Adjust the salt to taste:

Serves 4–6
Preparation: 30 minutes,
plus soaking
Cooking: approximately
1 1/4 hours

Ingredients
600 g/1 lb 5 oz basmati rice
5 tablespoons salt
100 g/3 1/2 oz fresh parsley
100 g/3 1/2 oz fresh dill
50 g/2 oz fresh coriander/
cilantro
100 g/3 1/2 oz fresh chives
4 cloves of garlic (or 4 sprigs of
fresh green garlic if available)
2 medium potatoes for the
tahdig (p. 131)
1 1/2 teaspoons turmeric
100 g/3 1/2 oz butter
3 tablespoons vegetable oil
2 tablespoons liquid saffron
(p. 28)

add more if not salty enough or rinse the rice if too salty. Fold the herb mixture into the rice in the colander, making sure the herbs are distributed evenly.

Return the saucepan to a medium heat. Melt 50 g/2 oz of butter and 2 tablespoons of oil and, when sizzling, cover the bottom of the saucepan with a layer of sliced potatoes. Sprinkle the rice mixture over the potatoes, starting from the centre of the pan and creating a pyramid, avoiding the sides of the pan. Take care not to break the grains of rice. Cut the remaining butter into small pieces and dot over the rice together with the rest of the oil. Wrap the lid in a clean tea towel and place firmly on the pan. Steam on a low heat (on a gas flame use the lowest setting and a heat diffuser) for 50 minutes to 1 hour. When you remove the lid the grains of rice should be thoroughly cooked and fluffy.

When the rice is ready, dip the bottom of the saucepan in the sink filled with 5 cm/2 inches of cold water for 1–2 minutes to loosen the crusty base layer (*tahdig*). Serve the rice onto a shallow dish, fluffing it up as you serve. Drizzle the saffron over the rice. Once the rice is removed the layer of crispy potatoes should come away from the bottom of the pan easily. Serve this on a separate plate.

This rice dish is so fresh and aromatic that it does not need many side dishes. Carrot and cumin salad (p. 176) and pickled garlic provide complementary flavours.

※

Saffron, yogurt and chicken 'upside down' rice

Tahchin ghalebi

Tahchin literally means 'arranged at the bottom' and refers to a layer of rice combined with meat to form a thick *tahdig*. Traditionally the rice is mixed with egg in addition to yogurt. *Tahchin* can be made with chicken or tender cuts of lamb; the chicken version is more popular and easier to make. There are also some vegetarian versions with spinach or aubergine/eggplant. This recipe is reasonably easy and the result is quite impressive. The thick Greek-style yogurt binds the rice together with the meat and when cooked in a heavy-based non-stick pan or a non-stick rice cooker you can turn it out like a cake onto your serving dish.

Preparation

Wash the rice and soak for 2 hours (see Preparation and soaking, p. 129).

Trim and wash the chicken thighs, remove the skin and bones, and pat the meat dry on kitchen paper. Peel and roughly chop the onion.

Cooking

Use a heavy-based saucepan, preferably non-stick, large enough to allow the rice and chicken pieces to be steamed together. Heat 2 tablespoons of oil and fry the onion until golden.

Add the chicken pieces and turmeric and stir well to seal the chicken on all sides. Add the lemon juice and 2 tablespoons of liquid saffron and season with salt and pepper. Reduce the heat, cover the pan and cook the chicken for approximately

Serves 4–6
Preparation: 25 minutes, plus soaking
Cooking: approximately 2 hours

Ingredients

600 g/1 lb 5 oz basmati rice

4 tablespoons salt

8 chicken pieces (preferably thighs)

1 large onion

4 tablespoons vegetable oil

½ teaspoon turmeric

3 tablespoons lemon juice

6 tablespoons liquid saffron (p. 28)

salt and black pepper

500 ml/just under 1 pint water

50 g/2 oz butter

400 g/14 oz Greek-style full-fat/whole milk yogurt

1 egg (optional)

30 minutes. When the chicken is cooked through, remove the pieces with a slotted spoon and set aside. Reserve the cooking juices in the pan.

Pour 500 ml/just under 1 pint of water into the pan with the chicken cooking juices. Add 1 tablespoon of salt and bring to the boil. Drain the rice and add to the pan with 1 tablespoon of oil and half of the butter. Simmer gently until all the water has been absorbed and small holes start to appear in the surface.

Mix the rest of the liquid saffron with the yogurt. Fold the saffron yogurt mixture and the chicken pieces into the rice, making sure that the chicken pieces are coated with the saffron yogurt.

Reduce the heat to a minimum (on a gas flame use the lowest setting and a heat diffuser), add the rest of the butter and the oil. Wrap the lid in a clean tea towel and place on the pan. Leave to steam for 1 hour.

Remove from the heat and stand the pan in 5 cm/2 inches of cold water for 1–2 minutes to loosen the crust before turning it upside down on a serving plate.

Tahchin goes well with *Salad-e Shirazi* (p. 181), cucumber and yogurt (p. 187), beetroot and yogurt (p. 190), pickles or chutney or a plate of fresh herbs (*Sabzi khordan*, p. 17/Chapter 1).

✳

OPPOSITE

Tahchin ghalebi. The flavours of chicken and saffron yogurt are concentrated in the crispy tahdig of this upside down rice.

Serves 4
Preparation: 20 minutes,
plus soaking
Cooking: approximately
1 1/4 hours

Ingredients

600 g/1 lb 5 oz basmati rice

3 tablespoons salt

150 g/5 oz *zereshk* (dried
barberries)

1 medium red onion

2 medium potatoes for the *tahdig*
(p. 131) (optional)

100 g/3 1/2 oz butter

100 ml/3 1/2 fl oz vegetable oil

4 tablespoons sugar

5 tablespoons liquid saffron
(p. 28)

20 g/ 3/4 oz pistachio slivers

20 g/ 3/4 oz almond slivers

500 ml/just under 1 pint water

OPPOSITE

*Top: Zereshk polo is an excellent
accompaniment to any dish.*

*Bottom: The crispy tahdig of Zereshk
polo is a feast for the eye as well as
the palate.*

Saffron barberry rice
Zereshk polo

The sweet and sour flavour of *zereshk* (barberries) and the
glistening ruby red berries set against the white and saffron-
tinged grains make this a feast for the taste buds and the
eyes. *Zereshk polo* is served at weddings and other celebrations
because it is impressive and easy to make in large quantities.
It is usually served with chicken, but it is also delicious with
Saffron yogurt lamb (p. 93) or Miniature meatballs (p. 108).

Although this recipe is neither time-consuming nor complicated,
you need to pay attention to cooking the berries before adding
them to the rice. When you buy dried barberries they should
have a bright red colour; the colour darkens with age and older
berries would adversely affect the taste and colour of your dish.

Preparation

Wash the rice and soak for 2 hours (see Preparation and
soaking, p. 129).

Spread the barberries on a tray and discard any that are spoilt
or discoloured. Pinch off any stalks remaining on the berries.
Wash the berries thoroughly in cold water. Soak briefly in cold
water then drain and pat dry on kitchen paper.

Peel and finely chop the onion. Wash, peel and thinly slice the
potatoes, if using, and put them in a bowl of cold water to
prevent discoloration.

Cooking

Heat 30 g/1 oz of the butter and 2 tablespoons of the oil in a
frying pan/skillet, add the onion and fry until golden. Reduce
the heat to low, add the barberries and stir; take care, as

barberries tend to burn very easily. Remove from the heat after a couple of minutes and add the sugar and 2 tablespoons of liquid saffron. Stir to dissolve the sugar and set aside.

Heat a small frying pan/skillet on a medium to low heat, add 1 tablespoon of oil and stir in the pistachios and almonds. Remove from the heat immediately. Add 1 tablespoon of the barberry mixture and 1 tablespoon of liquid saffron, stir and set aside.

Bring the water to the boil in a medium-sized, heavy-based saucepan. Drain the rice and add to the pan. Add 1 tablespoon of salt, 2 tablespoons of oil, 50 g/2 oz of butter and 1 tablespoon of liquid saffron. Bring back to the boil and simmer, uncovered, until all the water has been absorbed and holes appear on the surface of the rice.

Remove from the heat and tip the rice into a shallow dish. Gently fold in the barberry mixture, taking care not to break the grains of rice.

Rinse and return the saucepan to the heat. Add 2 tablespoons of oil and when it sizzles, line the bottom of the pan with a layer of sliced potatoes, if using. Spoon the barberry and rice mixture into the middle of the pan in a pyramid shape. Cut the rest of the butter into small pieces and dot over the rice. Wrap the lid in a clean tea towel and place it firmly on the pan. Leave to steam on a very low heat for 45–50 minutes.

When the rice is ready, dip the bottom of the pan in cold water. Fluff the rice as you serve it onto a shallow serving platter and decorate with the pistachio, almond and barberry mixture. Drizzle 1 tablespoon of liquid saffron over the top. Remove the *tahdig* in pieces and serve in a separate dish.

The light fruity taste of this dish goes well with most fresh salads.

TIP: The rice should be coloured by the saffron to a warm orange-yellow. If necessary you can add more liquid saffron to the rice as you are serving it.

Cumin saffron rice

Zireh polo

The addition of cumin seeds to plain rice makes it subtly aromatic
and a wonderful accompaniment to any chicken or fish dishes.

Preparation

Wash the rice and soak for 2 hours (see Preparation and
soaking, p. 129). Wash, peel and thinly slice the potato, if using,
and put the slices in a bowl of cold water.

Cooking

Bring the water to the boil in a medium-sized, heavy-based
saucepan. Drain the rice and add to the pan. Add 1 tablespoon
of salt, 2 tablespoons of oil and half of the butter. Bring back to
the boil and simmer, until all the water has been absorbed.

Tip the rice into a shallow bowl. To make a rice *tahdig* (instead
of potato), set aside 2 heaped tablespoons of the plain rice. Fold
the cumin seeds gently into the rest of the rice, taking care not
to break the grains of rice.

Return the saucepan to the heat. Add the remaining 1 tablespoon
of oil. When it sizzles, cover the bottom of the pan with the plain
rice you have set aside, or a layer of thinly sliced potato. Spoon
the cumin rice mixture into the middle of the pan in a pyramid
shape. Cut the rest of the butter into small pieces and dot over
the rice. Wrap the lid in a clean tea towel and place it firmly on
the pan. Leave to steam on a very low heat for 45–50 minutes.

When the rice is ready, dip the bottom of the pan in cold water.
Fluff the rice as you serve it onto a shallow serving platter.
Drizzle the saffron over the rice. Remove the *tahdig* in pieces
and serve on a separate plate.

Serves 4
Preparation: 15 minutes,
plus soaking
Cooking: approximately 1 hour

Ingredients
600 g/1 lb 5 oz basmati rice
4 tablespoons salt
1 large potato for the *tahdig*
(p. 131) (optional)
600 ml/1 pint water
2 tablespoons cumin seeds
3 tablespoons vegetable oil
50 g/2 oz butter
2 tablespoons liquid saffron
(p. 28)

Chapter 6

SALADS AND SIDE DISHES

Chapter 6

Salads and side dishes

S alads and yogurt dishes are an essential part of a Persian spread. No *sofreh* is complete without at least one or two yogurt side dishes and a plate of *Sabzi khordan*, a combination of fresh herbs such as mint, basil, tarragon, chives and watercress. These side dishes serve to cleanse the palate, prepare for a change of flavour or simply refresh the taste buds. They include yogurt mixed with vegetables and herbs, salads of all kinds, herbs and pickles. Pickles have not been included in this chapter but they are widely available in Persian and Middle Eastern shops.

Everything is brought to the table at the same time – *aashes*, *khoreshts*, rice dishes and side dishes – and meals are not divided into separate courses, but many of these side dishes can be served as a first course in a Western-style menu.

Depending on the occasion, a weekday family meal or a feast, side dishes may be simple and quickly prepared or more elaborate. At the very least, one would prepare a mixed salad, a small bowl of thick yogurt with a sprinkling of dried mint, and a little pickle to accompany an everyday meal. For a more formal occasion there would be one or more yogurt dishes, such as a *borani* (p. 182) or *Maast va khiar* (p. 187), a bouquet of fresh herbs (*Sabzi khordan*) with feta cheese and fresh bread, a salad or two and a few pickles.

OPPOSITE

Salad-e kasni va porteghal
(see p. 177).

PREVIOUS PAGES

An explosion of colours, textures and tastes in pomegranate salad.

Below: Onions, tomatoes and cucumbers are cut into small cubes to enhance the aroma and tastes of the ingredients in the Salad-e Shirazi (p. 181).

Traditionally, side dishes depended on the seasonal availability of herbs and vegetables, with a heavier emphasis on pickles and yogurt mixes in the winter and on salads and fresh herbs in the spring and summer. Nowadays with all-year-round availability of most foods there is less seasonal variation. These dishes help to maintain a balanced and healthy diet. From an early age, children develop the habit of eating yogurts, fresh vegetables and fruits with their meals.

Pomegranate, cucumber and red onion salad

Salad-e anar

This salad is a feast of colours and tastes, the ruby pomegranate grains complementing the green slices of cucumber and the purple colour of the onion. It can be eaten as a first course or to accompany a main meal. Pomegranate has become very popular in the West in recent years as a powerful antioxidant. The fruit and its bottled juice are now sold in most if not all supermarkets.

Preparation

Remove the seeds from the pomegranates (p. 23) and set aside.

If using small Middle Eastern cucumbers, slice them. Slice the onion thinly and separate the rings. If using larger cucumbers, chop them finely, and chop the onion finely.

Put the balsamic vinegar, sugar and olive oil in a small bowl and beat with a fork until thick and smooth. Season to taste. Stir in the onion and leave to stand for 15 minutes.

Add the pomegranate seeds and cucumber and mix thoroughly. Serve in a salad bowl and garnish with a sprig of mint.

Serves 4
Preparation: 30 minutes, plus standing time

Ingredients

2 pomegranates
100 g/3½ oz cucumber (p. 14)
1 red onion
1 tablespoon balsamic vinegar
½ teaspoon sugar
4 tablespoons extra virgin olive oil
salt and black pepper

Garnish

sprig of mint

See pp. 168-169 for recipe image.

Serves 4
Preparation: 30 minutes
Cooking: 30 minutes

Ingredients
1 orange, 1 yellow and 1 red
pepper
4 medium tomatoes
1 large red onion
4 cloves of garlic
4 tablespoons olive oil
1 head of red chicory/red endive
50 g/2 oz mixed salad leaves,
such as lamb's lettuce/corn salad
and rocket/arugula

Dressing
1 tablespoon balsamic vinegar
½ teaspoon sugar
4 tablespoons extra virgin
olive oil
a good pinch of chopped fresh
basil
salt and black pepper

Roast pepper salad
Salad-e felfel tanoori

This colourful salad is fragrant with the special aroma of roast
peppers mixed with garlic and olive oil. It is wonderful as a first
course or as a side dish with *Kotlet* (p. 115) and other main dishes.

Preparation
Preheat the oven to 220°C/425°F/gas mark 7. Wash the peppers
and dry them. Cut off the stems and cut the flesh into chunky
pieces, discarding the seeds. Wash and dry the tomatoes and cut
them in half. Peel the onion and cut into wedges.

Peel and crush the garlic. In a small bowl, mix the crushed
garlic with the olive oil. Wash the chicory and separate the
leaves. Wash the salad leaves and dry in a salad spinner.

Put the peppers, tomatoes and onions in a large roasting pan.
Drizzle with the olive oil and crushed garlic. Cook in the oven
for 30 minutes or until the peppers are brown at the edges.
Remove and set aside to cool.

Arrange the roasted vegetables in the middle of a large shallow
serving dish, with the chicory and salad leaves around them.
Put all the ingredients for the dressing in a small bowl and beat
with a fork until smooth. Pour the dressing over the vegetables
and toss thoroughly before serving.

Parsley and tomato salad
Salad-e ja'fari

Chopped parsley is wonderfully aromatic and goes well with tomato. This light and refreshing salad is an ideal side dish for most main courses, particularly *Lubia polo* (p. 151), *Tahchin* (p. 161) and *Kotlet* (p. 115).

Preparation
Wash the parsley in cold water and dry it in a salad spinner. Discard the thicker, tougher stalks. Using a sharp, wide-bladed knife, finely chop the leaves and tender stalks.

Cut the tomatoes in half and scoop out the seeds. Cut the flesh into strips and then cut them across to make tiny squares of tomato.

Wash and top and tail the spring onions/scallions and chop them finely.

For the dressing, mix the olive oil, lemon juice, salt and pepper in a salad bowl. Add the spring onions, mix with the dressing and let stand for about 10 minutes. Add the chopped tomatoes and parsley and mix thoroughly.

Serves 4
Preparation: 25 minutes, plus standing time

Ingredients
150 g/5 oz fresh flat-leafed parsley
300 g/11 oz tomatoes
3 spring onions/scallions

Dressing
4 tablespoons extra virgin olive oil
juice of 1 large lemon
salt and black pepper

TIP: For a refined version of this salad, skin the tomatoes before chopping them. Using a small, sharp knife, cut a cross in the base of each tomato. Put the tomatoes in a bowl of boiling water for about 1 minute, then rinse them under a cold tap. The skin should peel off easily.

Serves 4–6
Preparation: 10 minutes, plus
standing time

Ingredients
300 g/11 oz carrots
juice of 1 orange and 1 lemon
1 teaspoon sugar
1 heaped teaspoon cumin seeds
100 g/3½ oz raisins
salt and black pepper

Carrot and cumin salad
Salad-e haveej ba zireh

In this salad, raisins and cumin complement the flavour of carrots. It is great as an accompaniment to most fish dishes, such as *Mahi shekampor* (p. 100) and *Mahi ba gashneez* (p. 102).

Preparation
Grate the carrots.

In a salad bowl, mix the orange and lemon juice. Add the sugar, cumin seeds and raisins and season to taste. Let stand for 15 minutes so the raisins absorb the dressing. Add the grated carrots and mix thoroughly.

Chicory and orange salad

Salad-e kasni va porteghal

A delicate and fresh combination of tangy, juicy oranges, sweet, chewy raisins and the crisp bitterness of chicory/endive, enhanced by the lime dressing. Serve in a shallow dish to show off the vibrant colours. It is ideal as a first course before a fish main course, such as *Mahi shekampor* (p. 100).

Preparation
Trim off the base of the chicory/endive and remove the leaves, keeping them whole. Wash the leaves and dry them. Using a small, sharp knife, cut off the peel and pith of two of the oranges. Slice the flesh thinly and discard the pips.

Cut the remaining orange in half and squeeze the juice of one half into a small bowl. Add the lime juice, sugar, salt, pepper and olive oil. Beat with a fork until thick and smooth. In a separate bowl, mix the chicory/endive leaves, orange slices and raisins. Pour the dressing over and toss gently but thoroughly. Transfer to a shallow serving dish.

Serves 4–6
Preparation: 30 minutes

Ingredients
2 heads of chicory/endive: white, red or mixed
3 medium oranges
juice of 1 large lime
1 teaspoon sugar
salt and black pepper
4 tablespoons extra virgin olive oil
2 heaped tablespoons raisins

Above: Chicory and orange salad is an excellent starter or a flavoursome side salad to go with any dish.

Serves 4
Preparation: 25 minutes

Ingredients
2 large oranges
30 g/1 oz fresh flat-leafed parsley
1 fresh red chilli (or ½ teaspoon
dried red chilli flakes)
juice of 1 lemon
juice of ½ orange
1 teaspoon sugar
salt and black pepper
4 tablespoons extra virgin olive oil

Orange and parsley salad with chilli
Salad-e porteghal va ja'fari

The sweet and sour taste of this salad, combined with chilli, makes it ideal to serve after a main course to cleanse the palate.

Preparation

Using a small, sharp knife, cut off the peel and pith of the oranges. Chop the flesh into chunky pieces and discard the pips.

Wash the parsley in cold water and dry it in a salad spinner. Discard the thicker, tougher stalks. Using a sharp, wide-bladed knife, finely chop the leaves and tender stalks.

Wash and top and tail the chilli. Cut it lengthwise and scrape out the seeds with the blade of your knife, then chop the chilli finely.

Arrange the orange pieces in a shallow serving dish. Sprinkle the chilli and the parsley over.

In a small bowl, mix the lemon juice, orange juice, sugar, salt, pepper and olive oil. Beat with a fork until thick and smooth. Drizzle over the oranges just before serving.

Mixed vegetable salad
Salad-e makhloot

The combination of vegetables given here works well, but if one of the vegetables is unavailable, increase the amount of one of the others, or replace with a different vegetable, such as sugar snap peas or mangetout/snow peas. This salad is great as a first course or a side dish.

Preparation
Wash and trim the vegetables as necessary. Peel the carrot and cut into sticks. Blanch the vegetables separately for 2–3 minutes in a pan of boiling salted water.

They should remain firm to the bite: take care not to overcook them. Drain in a colander and cool rapidly in a bowl of iced water.

Mix all the ingredients for the dressing in a small bowl and whisk until smooth.

Mix the vegetables in a shallow serving dish, pour the dressing over and toss well.

Serves 4–6
Preparation: 15 minutes
Cooking: 10–15 minutes

Ingredients
100 g/3½ oz thin green beans
100 g/3½ oz asparagus tips
50 g/2 oz purple broccoli florets
50 g/2 oz cauliflower florets
50 g/2 oz carrot

Dressing
grated zest and juice of
½ a lemon
1 teaspoon creamed horseradish
(or mustard)
4 tablespoons extra virgin
olive oil
20 g/¾ oz chopped fresh mint
(optional)
salt and black pepper

VARIATION
Add lettuce or other green salad leaves to the mixture.

Cucumber, tomato and onion salad
Salad-e Shirazi

This salad is named after Shiraz, the city in the south of Iran famous for its beautiful gardens, poetry and wine. The fresh taste of tomatoes, cucumber, mint and lemon juice is very refreshing in the hot dry summer days in this part of the country. The ingredients are finely chopped to create an infusion of tastes in the lemon and olive oil dressing while maintaining their individual textures and tastes.

Preparation
Wash the tomatoes, cucumber and spring onions. Peel the onion. You can peel the cucumber and tomatoes for a more refined salad. Chop the vegetables finely.

Wash the herbs in cold water, dry thoroughly and chop finely.

Mix all the vegetables and fresh herbs in a deep salad bowl. Put the olive oil, lemon juice, dried mint, salt and pepper in a small bowl and beat with a fork until thick and smooth. Pour the dressing over the vegetables and mix thoroughly. It is best to make this salad about 1 hour before serving and keep it in the fridge to allow the flavours to marry.

Serves 4–6
Preparation: 25 minutes, plus chilling time

Ingredients
300 g/11 oz tomatoes
200 g/7 oz small, thin cucumbers (p. 14)
3 spring onions/scallions
1 medium red onion
1 tablespoon each of fresh parsley, tarragon and mint leaves
4 tablespoons extra virgin olive oil
juice of 1 large lemon
1 teaspoon dried mint
salt and black pepper

OPPOSITE
Light and refreshing, Salad-e Shirazi is the perfect accompaniment to any main dish.

Serves 4
Preparation: 20 minutes, plus
chilling time
Cooking: approximately
5 minutes

Ingredients

250 g/9 oz baby spinach

salt and black pepper

1 small onion

2 cloves of garlic

1 tablespoon olive oil

20 g/¾ oz walnuts

200 g/7 oz Greek-style full-fat/
whole milk yogurt

1 teaspoon dried mint

VARIATION

Replace spinach with the
succulent, nutritious leaves
of purslane. Chop 150 g/5 oz
of purslane (you don't need
to boil it) and add to the fried
onion and garlic mixture. Fry
briefly, then leave to cool and
follow the rest of the recipe.

OPPOSITE

The combination of creamy yogurt,
lightly fried baby spinach leaves and
crunchy walnuts is a healthy and
delicious mix.

Yogurt with spinach
Borani-e esfenaj

Borani consists of a cooked vegetable mixed with yogurt. There
are several variations, depending on the vegetables used and
whether herbs and garlic are included. The classic *borani* uses
spinach as the main vegetable, fried with onion and garlic. Left
to cool, and then chilled in the fridge, it is delicious as a first
course or a side dish.

Preparation

Wash the spinach, put it in a saucepan, add 125 ml/4 fl oz of
boiling water and 1 teaspoon of salt and cook for 5 minutes on
a medium-high heat. Remove with a slotted spoon and transfer
to a chopping board. Cut through the cooked spinach several
times with a sharp knife; set aside.

Peel the onion and garlic and chop finely. Heat the olive oil in
a small frying pan/skillet, add the onion and fry until golden
brown. Add the garlic and fry for 1 minute. Add the spinach,
stir to mix with the onion and the garlic, then remove from the
heat and leave to cool.

Chop the walnuts. In a serving bowl, mix the yogurt with the
walnuts and dried mint. Add the fried spinach, stir well, season to
taste and chill in the fridge for a couple of hours before serving.

Serves 4
Preparation: 10 minutes

Ingredients
150 g/5 oz heart of celery
30 g/1 oz walnuts
350 g/12 oz Greek-style full-fat/
whole milk yogurt
1 tablespoon lemon juice
salt and black pepper

Garnish
1 teaspoon dried mint
1 teaspoon walnuts, chopped

Celery and yogurt
Maast va karafs

The fresh aroma of chopped celery combines well with yogurt; walnuts add texture and their unique flavour. This salad goes well with most rice dishes and also with *Khoresht-e ghormeh sabzi* (p. 79). With crunchy fresh celery, creamy yogurt, walnuts and aromatic mint, it has a surprising diversity of textures.

Preparation
Wash and finely chop the celery. Chop the walnuts.

Put all the ingredients into a salad bowl (keep aside 1 tsp chopped walnuts for the garnish) and mix thoroughly. Taste and adjust the seasoning. Sprinkle on the garnish of dried mint and chopped walnuts. Keep in the fridge for up to 2 hours before serving.

OPPOSITE
Maast va karafs is a healthy and light side dish.

Cucumber and yogurt
Maast va khiar

This is a very popular dish, which is served as a dip and also as a side dish with almost all Persian dishes. In Iran they decorate the surface with aromatic dried rose petals (p. 26).

This recipe is slightly different from the traditional version as it uses other herbs in addition to mint. The cucumber should be chopped, not grated, to prevent the dish from becoming too watery.

Preparation
Chop the cucumber finely. Peel and grate the onion. Squeeze the grated onions to get rid of the juice and use just the pulp.

Mix all the ingredients thoroughly, taste and adjust the seasoning and serve immediately. It is important to mix the ingredients at the last minute since the mixture tends to become watery if allowed to stand.

Before serving sprinkle with aromatic dried rose petals (see chapter on Persian essentials p. 26).

Serves 4
Preparation: 15 minutes
Ingredients
250 g/9 oz cucumber, preferably the small Middle Eastern type (p. 14)
½ small red onion
200 g/7 oz Greek-style full-fat/ whole milk yogurt
1 teaspoon dried mint
a good pinch of chopped fresh herbs (parsley, tarragon, basil, chives)
1 tablespoon lemon juice
salt and black pepper

Garnish
Dried rose petals

VARIATION
Add coarsely chopped walnuts and raisins for a totally different taste.

OPPOSITE
The addition of rose petals as the garnish adds the heady hint of rose to maast va khiar.

Serves 4
Preparation: 15 minutes

Ingredients
1 large or 2 medium cooked
beetroots/beets
1 small clove of garlic
20 g/¾ oz walnuts
300 g/11 oz Greek-style full-fat/
whole milk yogurt
1 teaspoon dried mint
1 tablespoon lemon juice
1 teaspoon finely chopped fresh
tarragon (optional)
salt and black pepper

Beetroot and yogurt
Maast va laboo

Beetroots/beets, steamed or boiled, are a Persian winter staple. They are a good source of vitamin C and folic acid/folate, as well as iron, magnesium and other minerals, and in a recent study their unusually high nitrate levels have proven as effective as drugs in reducing blood pressure.

Beetroot is delicious on its own or in salads, boiled with a teaspoon of vinegar, and as an ingredient in yogurt dishes and *aashes*. This is an ideal accompaniment for meat and chicken dishes.

Preparation
Grate the beetroot into a bowl. Crush or finely chop the garlic. Chop the walnuts very finely.

Add the yogurt, garlic, walnuts, dried mint and lemon juice (and tarragon, if using) to the beetroot. Season to taste and mix thoroughly.

Keep in the fridge for no more than 1 hour before serving.

PREVIOUS PAGE
Sweet beetroot/beet grated and mixed with yogurt and topped with chopped tarragon laced with a hint of garlic; who can resist maast va laboo?

Russian salad
Salad Olivier

This is a variation of Russian potato salad; it is thought to be named after the chef who created it in Moscow in the 19th century. The recipe must have made its way south at some point and has been adapted to local tastes.

It is very popular in Iran and is sold in delicatessens as a filling for sandwiches; it is also made for big dinner parties or as part of the cold buffet at summer garden parties. It can be served as a meal on its own, or a smaller portion would serve as a first course; leave out the chicken for a vegetarian dish. It must be prepared in advance so that the dressing marries with the vegetables.

Preparation
Wash and dry the chicken. Peel the onion and cut into four wedges.

Heat the sunflower oil in a saucepan, add the onion and chicken and stir well to coat the onions and chicken in oil. Add the lemon juice and boiling water. Reduce the heat and simmer gently for 20–30 minutes or until the chicken is cooked. Set aside until cool and then shred the chicken.

Meanwhile, wash the potatoes. Boil in their skins until just tender, then drain, peel and set aside to cool. Chop them into 2 cm/¾ inch cubes.

Wash and peel the carrots. Boil them in salted water until just tender, then drain and set aside to cool. Chop them into 1 cm/½ inch cubes. Cook the peas in boiling salted water for 2 minutes, then drain and set aside.

Serves 6–8
Preparation: approximately 30 minutes, plus chilling time
Cooking: approximately 30 minutes

Ingredients
250 g/9 oz skinless chicken breast
1 small onion
2 tablespoons sunflower oil
2 tablespoons lemon juice
250 ml/9 fl oz boiling water
300 g/11 oz potatoes
100 g/3½ oz carrots
100 g/3½ oz green peas
100 g/3½ oz gherkins/cornichons
1 hard-boiled egg

Dressing
5 tablespoons mayonnaise
2 teaspoons mustard (any type)
4 tablespoons extra virgin olive oil
3 tablespoons lemon juice
salt and black pepper

Garnish
lemon slices
sliced gherkins/cornichons
green and black olives
1–2 tablespoons mayonnaise

Finely chop the gherkins/cornichons and the hard-boiled egg.

Prepare the dressing, in a small bowl, by whisking together the mayonnaise, mustard, olive oil, lemon juice and salt and pepper to taste.

Use a deep bowl, large enough to accommodate all the ingredients and have enough room for mixing.

Mix the potatoes, carrots, peas and shredded chicken with the chopped gherkins and egg; pour the dressing over. Using a large wooden spoon or your fingers, mix everything thoroughly. Leave in the fridge for a few hours.

Serve in a shallow dish. Decorate with slices of lemon and gherkin, olives, and a few teaspoons of mayonnaise.

☼

Yogurt drink
Doogh

Doogh, a refreshing drink made with yogurt, is the traditional drink of choice with most Persian dishes. It has been included in this chapter because it generally accompanies meals and until recently was rarely offered as a drink on its own.

In Iran you can buy yogurt that is naturally slightly sour in taste. Here I have suggested adding lemon or lime juice to achieve the same result. The proportion of yogurt to water is a matter of personal taste: I use one part yogurt to four parts water, but you may prefer a thicker or thinner drink.

Preparation
Put the yogurt in a large jug and add the still or sparkling water, stir until evenly blended and add salt and pepper to taste. You can add a few drops of lemon juice for a tangier drink.

Serve chilled or with added ice cubes. Sprinkle some dried mint on top if you like.

Serves 4
Preparation: 5 minutes, plus chilling time

Ingredients
250 g Greek-style full-fat/whole milk yogurt
1 litre/1¾ pints cold water (or sparkling mineral water)
salt and black pepper
1 tablespoon lime juice (or lemon juice) (optional)
2 teaspoons dried mint (optional)

Chapter 7

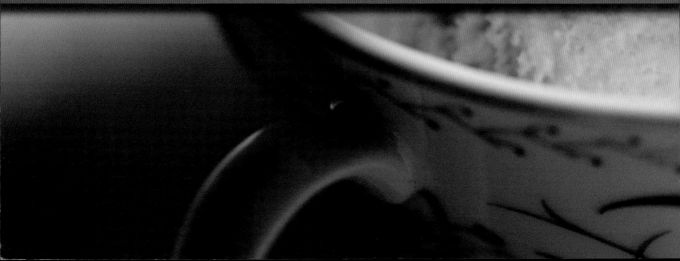

DESSERTS

Chapter 7

Desserts

Iranians usually finish a meal with tea (drunk without milk) accompanied by fruit or sweets such as dates, baklava or *noghl* (sugared almond slivers). These sweets are widely available in Middle Eastern shops in the West. Persian meals, being less structured into courses than in the West, do not have the tradition of a dessert course. However, as Iranian households become more westernized, the sweet dishes that have always been a part of Persian fare are increasingly being served as Western-style desserts. Ice creams and sorbets, plentiful in Iran, and usually eaten as snacks in the afternoon or summer evenings, are now often served after a meal. This chapter includes a variety of ice creams, fruit dishes and sweetmeats to complement a Persian dinner.

Paloodeh, or rice noodle sorbet, is a Persian favourite, but the noodles are rarely seen in the West and are not the easiest things to make! The most famous version of *paloodeh* comes from Shiraz. The city has special cafés, like ice cream parlours, that serve *paloodeh* with fresh Shirazi lime juice. Some people prefer to add rose water, orange blossom water, morello cherry juice or other fruit juices. They make great thirst-quenchers in the hot summer days of Shiraz.

Ice cream in Iran is wonderfully creamy and viscous because of one of its ingredients, *sa'lab*, or salep, a white powder derived

from certain types of orchid. This is not widely available in the West, so we have created some delicious ice cream recipes that don't need salep. Whereas in the West you find all manner of solid bits mixed into ice cream, from chocolate to praline to cookie dough, traditional Persian ice creams often include pieces of clotted cream for a contrast in texture and flavour.

For the three ice cream recipes and the Paloodeh an ice cream maker will speed up the process and produce better results. If you don't have one, use the 'tray method': pour the ice cream mix into a chilled freezer container (preferably shallow) and freeze for two hours until mushy. Then turn into a chilled bowl and beat well. Return to the freezer and freeze until firm. Transfer to the fridge to soften 30 minutes before serving. All ice creams can be made up to two or three days in advance and stored in the freezer, but must be taken out of the freezer before serving, then stirred to regain their smooth texture. They are delicious served with fresh berries.

Right: Intensely nutty and sweet with the aroma of rose water, Baklava is a traditional sweet to eat with tea.

Orange blossom and cinnamon ice cream

Bastani-e bahar-narenj

Orange blossom water flavours many sweets in Iran. This light and aromatic ice cream is easy to make and is particularly refreshing after a fish or lamb main course.

Cooking

Put the milk and cream in a saucepan and bring to the boil. Add the cinnamon stick. Reduce the heat and simmer gently, stirring frequently, until the liquid is reduced by about a quarter (stirring will prevent it from boiling over). This should take 20–25 minutes and the liquid will turn a creamy colour. Remove from the heat and strain through a sieve; discard the cinnamon. Leave to cool for 15 minutes.

Meanwhile, put the sugar and orange blossom water in a small saucepan on a low heat and stir to dissolve the sugar. Simmer the liquid until it forms a thin syrup (approximately 10 minutes). Remove from the heat and leave to cool for 10–15 minutes.

In a bowl combine the milk and cream mixture, the orange blossom syrup and the evaporated milk. Chill in the fridge for at least 2 hours, preferably overnight.

Churn in an ice cream maker following the manufacturer's instructions or make according to the tray method (see p. 198).

Serves 4–6
Preparation: 5 minutes, plus cooling and churning
Cooking: approximately 30–35 minutes

Ingredients
600 ml/1 pint full-fat/whole milk
600 ml/1 pint double/heavy cream
1 cinnamon stick
150 g/5 oz sugar
225 ml/8 fl oz orange blossom water
400 ml/14 fl oz unsweetened evaporated milk

Serves 4–6
Preparation: 10 minutes, plus
cooling and churning
Cooking: 20–30 minutes

Ingredients

120 g/4 oz pistachio slivers, plus
extra to decorate
150 g/5 oz sugar
600 ml/1 pint full-fat/whole
milk
600 ml/1 pint double/heavy
cream
400 ml/14 fl oz unsweetened
evaporated milk

Pistachio ice cream

Bastani-e pesteh

This ice cream has a subtle nutty flavour and a delightful pale green colour. A wonderful finish to most Persian meals.

Preparation

Put the pistachios and sugar in a blender and reduce to a fine powder.

Cooking

Put the milk, cream, and sugar and pistachio mixture in a saucepan and bring to the boil. Reduce the heat and simmer gently, stirring frequently, until the liquid is reduced by about a quarter (stirring will prevent it from boiling over and extract the maximum flavour from the nuts). This should take 20–30 minutes. The liquid will turn green.

Remove from the heat and leave to cool for 15 minutes. Strain through a fine sieve to remove the nuts, squeezing the liquid from the nuts by pressing with the back of a spoon. Discard the nut residue. Combine the pistachio cream with the evaporated milk. Chill in the fridge for at least 2 hours, preferably overnight.

Churn in an ice cream maker following the manufacturer's instructions or make according to the tray method (see p. 198). Sprinkle with pistachio slivers to serve.

Saffron ice cream
Bastani-e za'farani

Persian cuisine uses saffron extensively in both sweet and savoury dishes. Its unique aroma and colour gives this ice cream a distinctive flavour and appearance. It is a very quick and easy ice cream to make, best served after fish or chicken dishes.

Cooking

Put the milk, cream, saffron and sugar in a large saucepan. Bring to the boil, stirring to dissolve the sugar and the saffron. Reduce the heat and simmer gently, stirring frequently, until the liquid is reduced by about a quarter (20–25 minutes). Add the evaporated milk and chill in the fridge for at least 2 hours, preferably overnight. Churn in an ice cream maker following the manufacturer's instructions or make according to the tray method (see p. 198).

Serves 4–6
Preparation: 5 minutes, plus cooling and churning
Cooking: 20–25 minutes

Ingredients
600 ml/1 pint full-fat/whole milk
600 ml/1 pint double/heavy cream
large pinch of ground saffron (p. 27)
150 g/5 oz sugar
400 ml/14 fl oz unsweetened evaporated milk

Above: Delicately flavoured and elegantly colourful saffron ice cream.

Serves 4–6
Preparation: 30 minutes, plus chilling time

Ingredients

1 ripe melon

2–3 kiwi fruit

½ pineapple

1 large ripe mango (or papaya)

2 blood oranges (or regular oranges)

100 g/3½ oz seedless grapes

juice of 1 lemon

2 teaspoons sugar

a dash of Grand Marnier (optional)

100 g/3½ oz mulberries (or raspberries or blackberries)

Seven-fruit salad
Salad-e haft miveh

Persians like to end the meal with fruits as they are considered to aid digestion. *Haft miveh* means seven fruits; the idea is to have a colourful combination of fruits – you don't necessarily need to have seven. This fruit salad goes very well with vanilla ice cream or crème fraîche. For a Western twist, you can add a little Grand Marnier for aroma and kick!

Preparation

Cut the melon into 2 cm/¾ inch cubes, discarding the skin. Peel and slice the kiwi fruit. Cut the pineapple and mango or papaya into 2–4 cm/approximately 1 inch cubes, discarding the skin. Using a small sharp knife, cut the skin and pith off the oranges and cut them into small wedges.

In a large, preferably clear, salad bowl mix the lemon juice and sugar and the Grand Marnier, if using. Fold in all the fruits except the mulberries. Mix thoroughly. Chill in the fridge for at least 2 hours.

Just before serving add the berries; gently fold them in so that they don't get bruised.

Caramelized pineapple

Caramel-e ananas

To make this dessert, you can caramelize almost any fruit: banana, mango, orange, peach, pear, pineapple, plum, apple, strawberries. The most popular, however, is pineapple, which caramelizes very well and is believed to aid digestion, so is perfect to round off a meal.

Preparation

With a sharp knife, cut the pineapple into slices 1 cm/½ inch thick, then remove the skin from each slice (you can remove the central core for a more refined dish).

Cooking

In a heavy-based frying pan/skillet on a medium heat, melt the butter and sugar together. (If you are using softer fruit, let the butter and sugar bubble together for 3 minutes, stirring frequently.) Arrange the fruit in the pan and cook until the fruit begins to turn brown (approximately 10 minutes). Turn to caramelize both sides. Serve with whipped cream or ice cream.

Serves 4–6
Preparation: 10 minutes
Cooking: 10 minutes (less if using softer fruits)

Ingredients
1 ripe pineapple
50 g/2 oz unsalted butter
50 g/2 oz sugar (white or brown)

TIPS: If the fruit is not ripe enough, add a little more sugar to compensate. Softer fruit such as strawberries and bananas need less cooking (approximately 1–2 minutes), so you should let the butter and sugar caramelize before adding the fruit.

Serves 6–8
Preparation: 5 minutes plus
cooling
Cooking: approximately
15 minutes

Ingredients

120 g/4 oz sugar

100 ml/3½ fl oz rose water

½ teaspoon ground saffron
(p. 27)

100 g/3½ oz plain/all-purpose
flour

3 tablespoons vegetable oil

50 g/2 oz unsalted butter

TIP: It is important to get
the colour of the flour right.
If the flour is left for too long
on the heat and turns brown,
the halva will taste burnt.
When the mixture is viscous,
remove from the heat and
keep stirring.

Bushehri dessert

Halva Bushehri

Halva is a very sweet, aromatic dessert. Recipes differ
depending on the region. This version, from Bushehr on the
Persian Gulf, is referred to as '*angosht peech*', meaning that it is
so viscous that you can wrap it around your finger like a thread!
Unlike the better-known version of halva, a firm sweet based
on ground sesame seeds, this version is eaten with a spoon.
The secret of a good halva is the precise cooking of the flour:
it needs careful attention to ensure it's removed from the heat
when the flour is golden brown, but before it turns dark brown.

Cooking

Put the sugar, rose water and saffron in a small saucepan on a
very low heat until the sugar dissolves. Set aside and cover to
keep warm.

Mix the flour, oil and butter in another saucepan on a medium
heat until the flour turns golden brown (not dark brown),
stirring frequently to make a smooth paste; this should take
approximately 10 minutes.

Remove from the heat and very slowly add the warm rose water
and sugar mixture, stirring all the time; return to a very low
heat, stirring continually for approximately 5 minutes, to create
a smooth viscous paste. Remove from the heat and keep stirring
for another couple of minutes. Pour into a shallow dish and
smooth and flatten the surface with a wooden spatula. Set aside
to cool at room temperature.

Stuffed dates with walnuts
Ranginak

This is a very rich dessert, usually made in winter months. The dates for this dessert are called *rotab* in Iran; they are fresh, soft and light brown in colour and you can find them in good Middle Eastern shops. The boxed dried dates commonly found in supermarkets are not suitable for *ranginak*. You can, however, use medjool dates instead of *rotab*.

Preparation
Stone/pit the dates and stuff each date with quarter of a walnut. Arrange the stuffed dates in a flat dish, side by side in rows and nestling together.

Cooking
Melt the butter in a frying pan on a medium heat, stir in the flour, and continue cooking and stirring until the flour turns golden brown and the mixture has a creamy consistency. Pour the mixture over the dates. Sprinkle with the pistachio and almond mixture and the cinnamon. Leave to cool at room temperature before serving.

Serves 6
Preparation: 10–15 minutes plus cooling
Cooking: 10 minutes

Ingredients
500 g/1 lb 2 oz *rotab* dates (or medjool dates)
100 g/3½ oz walnut halves
100 g/3½ oz unsalted butter
200 g/7 oz plain/all-purpose flour
1 teaspoon mixed ground pistachios and almonds
a pinch of ground cinnamon

Saffron rice pudding
Sholleh zard

Sholleh zard is traditionally made for festive and religious occasions. Its subtle flavouring makes this an ideal dessert after a light meal.

Preparation

Cut the almonds into slivers and crush the pistachios. If using cardamom, slit the pods, remove the seeds and grind them with a pestle and mortar.

Cooking

Put the rice, salt and water into a heavy-based saucepan on a medium heat and bring to the boil. Boil until the rice is thoroughly cooked and the mixture is thick.

Add the sugar and bring back to the boil, stirring continually. Add the liquid saffron and the rose water; stir well, then add the almonds, cardamom and butter and stir to mix thoroughly. Cover with a lid, reduce the heat to minimum and cook for a further 40–50 minutes, stirring occasionally.

Remove from the heat and pour into serving bowls. Leave to cool at room temperature. Decorate with cinnamon and crushed pistachios.

Serves 6–8
Preparation: 10 minutes plus cooling
Cooking: approximately 1 ¼ hours

Ingredients
20 g/¾ oz almonds
20 g/¾ oz pistachios
200 g/7 oz rice (any type)
½ teaspoon salt
2 litres/3½ pints water
400 g/14 oz sugar
2 tablespoons liquid saffron (see p. 28)
3 tablespoons rose water
2–3 green cardamom pods (optional)
50 g/2 oz unsalted butter
1 teaspoon ground cinnamon

OPPOSITE
A beautifully decorated dish of sholleh zard, *pleasing to the eye and promising a feast of sweet creamy rice mixed with almonds and pistachios.*

Makes 1–1.2 kg/
approximately 2½ lb
Preparation: 10 minutes
Cooking: approximately 1 hour

Ingredients
500 g/1 lb 2 oz quinces
250 ml/9 fl oz water
650 g/1 lb 7 oz granulated sugar
5 cardamom pods

Quince jam and yogurt
Morabba va maast

Yogurt makes a delicious dessert when served with jam; quince jam is particularly tasty. Quinces are popular throughout the Middle East and around the Mediterranean and are used in both sweet and savoury dishes. Although less common further north, the fragrant fruit, looking like a lumpy, pale golden apple with a light covering of down, can often be found in Middle Eastern stores and farmers' markets in late summer. This jam is a lovely way to capture their scent and colour.

Preparation
Sterilize your jam jars.

Peel the quinces and set the peel aside. Cut each fruit into four wedges, remove the seeds and slice each wedge thinly. Wrap the peel in a piece of clean muslin/cheesecloth.

Cooking
Put the quince slices in heavy-based saucepan, add the water and boil for 15 minutes. Add the sugar, reduce the heat and stir well. Put the cloth containing the quince peel on top, cover the pan and simmer until the water is reduced by half and the quince pulp is bright red; this should take about 20–30 minutes.

Add the cardamom pods, stir and let the jam simmer for a further 15 minutes. Remove from the heat and let the jam cool before transferring to the jars.

Serve Greek-style yogurt in ice cream dishes or martini glasses with a blob of the ruby red quince jam on top.

Noodle sorbet

Paloodeh shirazi

Noodle sorbet is very popular throughout Iran and the version from the city of Shiraz is the most famous.

Cooking

Make a sugar syrup by putting the sugar and water in a saucepan. Set over a low heat and stir frequently until the sugar dissolves. Bring to the boil, and let it boil for 5–8 minutes. Cool quickly over ice, or leave to cool and then chill in the fridge for 4–5 hours.

Cut the noodles into pieces about 2 cm/¾ inch long and place in a heatproof bowl. Add boiling water to cover and leave for 5 minutes or until soft. Set aside to cool down. Put the syrup into an ice cream maker and churn following the manufacturer's instructions or make according to the tray method (see p. 198).

Just before serving, mix the prepared noodles with the frozen syrup. Serve immediately in ice cream glasses with a teaspoon of rose water or essence of orange blossom or few drops of lime juice. Decorate the paloodeh with fresh lime wedges, pomegranate seeds or a spoonful of cherry jam.

Serves 4
Preparation: 5 minutes, plus cooling and churning
Cooking: approximately 10 minutes

Ingredients

250 g/9 oz granulated sugar
400 ml/14 fl oz water
40 g/1½ oz fine rice noodles (vermicelli)
4 teaspoons rose water or orange blossom water (or fresh lime juice)
fresh lime wedges, pomegranate seeds or cherry jam to decorate

Above: Paloodeh shirazi is a refreshing sweet sorbet with the tang of pomegranate seeds and lime.

Chapter 8

DRINKS

Chapter 8

Drinks

Hot drinks

Tea

Tea is the traditional hot drink of Iran, drunk morning, noon and night in small, slender, elegant glasses (*istikans*), often encased in a silver holder. It is never drunk with milk. For more than 100 years, India has exported some of its highest grade Darjeeling tea to Iran, although Iran produces its own tea along its Caspian coastline.

The best way to take tea the traditional Iranian way is to treat yourself to pure Darjeeling leaves. They produce a pale tea, with a strong flavour and beguiling perfume. In Iran, tea is generally brewed in a porcelain teapot rather than a metallic one. Heat the pot first, then add the tea leaves. Add the water a few seconds before it comes to the boil, or wait until the water is settled (not boiling any more), to allow the leaves to come to life gently: boiling water kills the flavour. Darjeeling tea is usually brewed for about 10 minutes, with a single stir halfway through brewing. Blends that include Assam and Ceylon teas require less brewing time.

The pot is placed on a samovar to keep the water and tea mixture at a constant temperature as it brews. Given that samovars are increasingly rare in Iranian homes, and

OPPOSITE

Detail of the interior of the music room in one of the palaces in Esfahan.

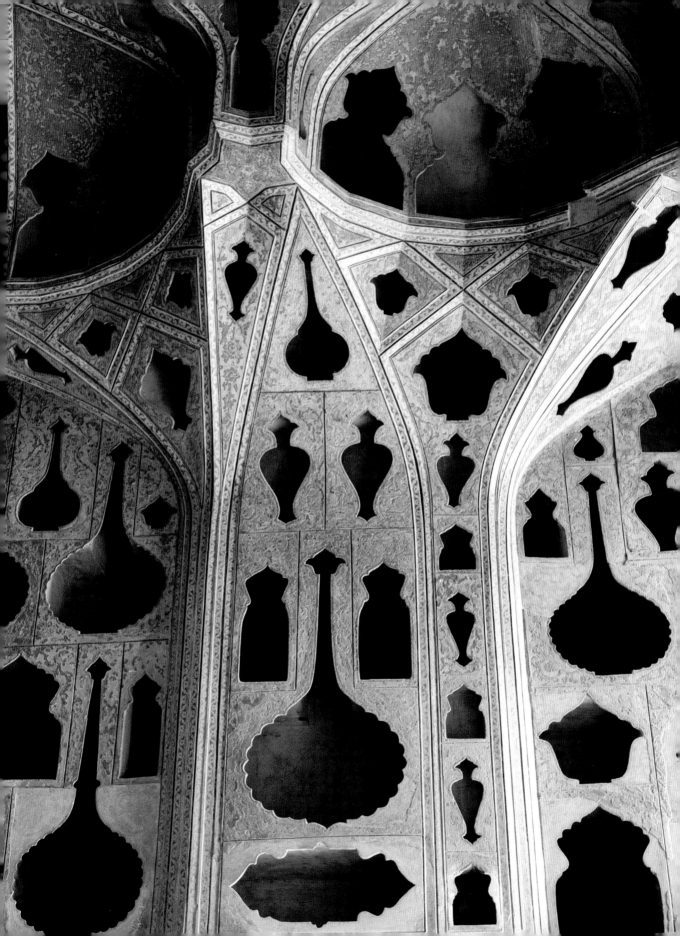

non-existent in the West, the same effect can be achieved by placing the pot on an equally gentle source of heat, such as a warming plate or an electric hob on a very low heat, and covering the pot with a tea cosy.

In order to show its deep amber colour to best effect, the tea is always served in a glass rather than a cup or mug. The tea may be diluted to taste with boiling water, and is usually accompanied by sweets, baklava or similar delicacies. Rather than adding sugar, some prefer to put sugar lumps in their mouths and suck the tea through the lumps.

Herbal teas, generally favoured for their medicinal properties, are also popular in Iran. Varieties include camomile, cinnamon, ginger, mint, orange blossom and valerian.

Torsh

This hot, fruit-based drink was once very popular in Iran, and it seems to be coming back into favour. Though the word '*torsh*' means sour in Persian, the drink was usually sweetened with sugar. To make *torsh*, use one measure of water to half a measure of fruit: for example 1 cup of water, ½ cup of fruit and 1 teaspoon of sugar per serving. Some fruits are boiled in water and some are brewed like tea.

Torsh-e albaloo (sour cherries)
In a small pan, boil the fresh sour cherries and sugar in water until they are soft and the water has turned red. Pass through a sieve and adjust the sugar to taste before serving.
If you are using frozen cherries, put them in a sieve to thaw at room temperature. Use as above once thawed.

Torsh-e seeb (sour apples)
Choose crunchy tart apples for this recipe. Wash, core and chop the apples. Add 2 teaspoons of lemon juice per ½ cup of

chopped apple. Boil until the apple is soft. Pass through a sieve and add sugar to taste before serving.

Torsh-e beh (quince)

This *torsh* is brewed rather than boiled. Wash, core and finely chop the quince, add one slice of lemon per $\frac{1}{2}$ cup of quince. Put the mixture in a teapot and add boiling water. Leave on a samovar or very low heat to brew for a few minutes. Pass through a sieve and add sugar to taste before serving.

Cold drinks

Sharbats

Traditionally, jars of fruit syrups, or *sharbats*, prepared when the fruit was in season, could be found lining the shelves of the cellar in every house in anticipation of the summer heat. For everyday use, jugs of ice-cold diluted *sharbat* would be made and kept in the fridge. When visiting family and friends in the hot days of summer in Iran, you would always be welcomed with a tray of ice-cold *sharbats*, colourful and thirst-quenching. We have chosen some of the most popular variations, but the possibilities are endless. There is a case to be made for replacing tea and coffee with *sharbat* during the warmer months of the year, wherever you might be; they're certainly a healthier alternative to today's ubiquitous fizzy drinks.

When serving a *sharbat*, you can layer the liquids one on top of the other without stirring. Take a tall glass. Pour in ice-cold water to come two-thirds of the way up, then gently pour in 1–2 tablespoons of the sweet syrup. The syrup should sink to the bottom and settle in a layer. Add two or three ice cubes. Serve with a long teaspoon or a straw. Once you have constructed your delicate drink in striking or subtle stripes, your guest will have the pleasure of stirring it to see the colours mix and change. This also allows them to mix as much or as little of the syrup with the ice water as they like.

Sugar syrup

For some *sharbats* and almost all *araq* (p. 218) drinks you need sugar syrup. Sugar syrup provides instant sweetness and gives a crystal-clear drink. It is worth making a small bottle of sugar syrup to keep in the fridge throughout the summer months. Measuring by volume, use half as much water as sugar, for example 1 cup of water to 2 cups of sugar. Pour the water and sugar into a pan and place on a low heat. Let the sugar dissolve in the water and the mixture come to a gentle boil. Stir occasionally. Leave it to simmer for a few minutes, then take off the heat and let it cool.

Sharbat-e ablimoo (lime juice)

Although lemon juice can be used for this *sharbat*, lime juice is preferred because of its heavenly aroma and wicked sharpness. When extracting the juice, try to get some of the lime pulp out to add to the flavour. Add 1 tablespoon of sugar syrup to 2–3 tablespoons of lemon or lime juice.

Sharbat-e albaloo (sour cherries)

You may come across fresh sour cherries in season; frozen morello cherries are available all year round from some supermarkets.

Stone and weigh the cherries and put them in a saucepan with double the weight of sugar (for example 500 g/1 lb 2 oz cherries to 1 kg/2¼ lb sugar). Let them gently simmer on a low heat until the sugar is completely dissolved and the cherries are softened and cooked (approximately 20–30 minutes).

To test the consistency, take a teaspoon of the cherry syrup and pour it onto a saucer; leave it to cool for a couple of minutes. The liquid should be thick but you should be able to move it around the saucer. If it is too thin, let the mixture simmer for a little longer (it should not have the consistency of jam because you need to separate the liquid from the fruit to make the *sharbat*). Remove the pan from the heat. Let the mixture drip through muslin for several hours until all the syrup is separated from the fruit.

Just before removing the pan from the heat, some cooks add a couple of drops of vanilla essence to the cherry mixture.

Sekanjabin

This sweet and sour syrup is made with vinegar, sugar and water. The recipe is best measured by volume: two of sugar to one of water and half of white wine vinegar. Let the water and sugar come to a gentle boil for a few minutes before adding the vinegar. Stir and add a few sprigs of fresh mint. Simmer for a few minutes longer. Take off the heat and strain into a clean jar. Leave to cool.

To serve, pour ice-cold water into the glass, then gently pour in the syrup.

Sharbat-e khiar sekanjabin

Make *Sekanjabin* as above. To serve, pour ice-cold water into the glass, add 2 teaspoons (or as much as 2 tablespoons) of grated cucumber then gently pour in the *Sekanjabin* and add a small sprig of mint. The crunchiness of the cucumber with the chewy and aromatic mint and the sweet and sour syrup combines to make an effective thirst-quencher of a drink!

TIP: If you cannot obtain fresh or frozen cherries, you can use the syrup from morello cherry jam as the base for a cherry *sharbat*.

Araqiyat

These are fragrant, refreshing drinks made from a combination of sugar syrup, water and flower or herbal essences. In Iran, there are special cafés that serve these drinks and have an extensive stock of different essences, which are said to cure various ailments, from nerves to fever! These four delicious versions are made with extracts that are readily available in Middle Eastern supermarkets. The amount of sugar syrup and flower or herbal essence you use is a matter of personal taste.

Araq-e bahar narenj (orange blossom)
Take a tall glass and fill three-quarters full with ice-cold water. Add 2–4 teaspoons of sugar syrup (p. 216), 1 teaspoon of orange blossom water and a couple of ice cubes and stir to mix.

Araq-e na'na (mint)
Take a tall glass and fill three-quarters full with ice-cold water. Add 2–4 teaspoons of sugar syrup (p. 216), 1 teaspoon of mint essence and a couple of ice cubes and stir to mix. Add a mint leaf to the glass before serving.

Sharbat-e golab (rose water)
Take a tall glass and fill three-quarters full with ice-cold water. Add 2–4 teaspoons of sugar syrup (p. 216), 1 teaspoon of edible rose water and a couple of ice cubes and stir to mix. Decorate with one or two edible rose petals.

Araq-e kasni (chicory/endive)
Take a tall glass and fill three-quarters full with ice-cold water. Add 2–4 teaspoons of sugar syrup (p. 216), 1 teaspoon of chicory/endive essence and a couple of ice cubes. Stir to mix.

Other cold drinks

Ab-e anar (freshly squeezed pomegranate juice) is very refreshing and is a popular drink in Iran when pomegranates are in season, from late summer through to December. Most of the pomegranate drinks available in Western supermarkets contain concentrated pomegranate juice, sugar and other fruit juices, so it is worth making your own – and it is not difficult.

Use a juicer, or alternatively roll the pomegranates firmly on a hard surface to crush the seeds, then cut each pomegranate in half over a bowl to catch the juice; squeeze out the remaining juice, and strain to remove pieces of bitter pith. Two medium pomegranates will produce about 250 ml/9 fl oz of juice.

Doogh (p.193), a drink made from yogurt, is served to accompany meals, rather than being offered as simple refreshment.

Bibliography

Web addresses were correct at the time of writing.

Abbott, Jacob, *History of Alexander the Great*, Nathaniel Cooke, London, 1853

Carter, Charles, *The Compleat City and Country Cook: or Accomplish'd Housewife*, London, 1732 (http://www.archive.org/stream/compleatcityandoocartgoog)

Daryabandari, Najaf, *Ketab-e Mostatab-e Ashpazi Az Seer Ta Piaz*, Karnameh Press, Tehran, 2000

Emami, Goli, *Ashpazi Bedoon-e Goosht*, Niloofar Press, Tehran, 1990

Hazlitt, W. Carew, *Old Cookery Books and Ancient Cuisine*, Elliot Stock, 62 Paternoster Row, London, 1886

Herodotus, *Persian Wars Book 7 – Polymnia* (translated by George Rawlinson 1942, edited by Bruce J. Butterfield) (http://www.parstimes.com/history/herodotus/persian_wars/polymnia.html)

Joret, Charles, *Les Plantes dans l'Antiquité et au Moyen Age, II l'Iran et l'Inde*, Emile Bouillon, Paris, 1904 (http://www.archive.org/details/lesplantesdanslo1joregoog)

Joret, Charles, *La Rose dans l'Antiquité et au Moyen Age*, Emile Bouillon, Paris, 1892 (http://www.archive.org/details/larosedanslantioojoregoog)

C. Kole (Ed), *Genome Mapping and Molecular Breeding in Plants, Volume 4, Fruits and Nuts*, Springer Verlag, Berlin and Heidelberg, 2007

Laufer, Berthold, *Sino-Iranica; Chinese Contributions to the History of Civilization in Ancient Iran*, Chicago, 1919 (www.archive.org/stream/sinoiranicachineoolaufrich)

McCormick Spices of the World Cookbook (prepared and tested by Mary Collins), Penguin, 1974

Montazami, Roza, *Honar-e Ashpazi*, Iran Chaap, Tehran, 1969

Moore, Thomas, *Lallah Rookh*, Longman, Rees, Orme, Brown and Green, London, 1826

Murray, Hugh, F.R.S.E, *Travels of Marco Polo*, Oliver & Boyd, Tweeddale Court, Edinburgh, 1844

Neshatoddowleh, Banoo, *Tabbakhi Neshat*, Mesbahi, Tehran, 1972

Roden, Claudia, *A New Book of Middle Eastern Food*, Penguin, 1986

Shaida, Margaret, *The Legendary Cuisine of Persia*, Grub Street, London, 2004

This, Hervé and Gagnaire, Pierre, *Cooking, the Quintessential Art*, University of California Press, 2008

Glossary

Aabdoogh khiar (p. 51) – chilled cucumber soup with yogurt and herbs

Aash – a thick soup

Aash-e anar (p. 41) – herb and pomegranate soup

Aash-e jo (p. 43) – barley and herb soup

Aash-e maast (p. 45) – dill, mint and yogurt soup

Aash-e sholleh ghalamkar (p. 48) – mixed pulses and herb soup

Abgusht (p. 39) – lamb soup with pulses

Adas polo (p. 136) – Rice with green lentils, raisins and dates

Advieh – spice blend

Albaloo – sour cherry

Albaloo polo (p. 139) – Sour cherry rice

Araq-e bahar narenj (p. 218) – orange blossom essence used to make a cold drink

Araq-e na'na (p. 218) – mint essence used to make a cold drink

Araq-e kasni (p. 218) – chicory/ endive essence used to make a cold drink

Araqiyat – essence of flowers or herbs

Badenjan – aubergine

Baghala pokhteh – Broad beans boiled in the pod

Baghala polo (p. 141) – Broad beans and dill rice

Barbari – thick flat bread

Barreh za'farani (p. 93) – Saffron yogurt lamb

Bastani-e bahar-narenj (p. 199) Orange blossom and cinnamon ice cream

Bastani-e pesteh (p. 200) Pistachio ice cream

Bastani-e za'farani (p. 201) Saffron ice cream

Beh – quince

Borani – a yogurt and vegetable dish

Borani-e esfenaj (p. 182) – yogurt with spinach

Caramel-e ananas (p. 203) Caramelized pineapple

Chelo (p. 134) – plain white rice

Chelo kabab – chargrilled lamb served with rice

Chelo kabab barg (p. 103) – kebab made from fillet of lamb or beef

Dampokhtak – rice cooked with pulses

Dampokhtak-e baghala (p. 144) – Sticky rice with yellow beans and dill

Dolmeh (p. 119) – stuffed vegetables

Dom siah – 'black tail', a type of rice

Doogh (p. 193) – yogurt drink

Eshkeneh (p. 52) – fenugreek soup

Ghalyeh mahi (p. 75) – khoresht of fish with coriander

Ghalyeh maygoo (p. 76) – khoresht of prawns with coriander (variation)

Gheimeh – small pieces of meat – see *Khoresht-e gheimeh*

Ghormeh sabzi – see *Khorest-e ghormeh sabzi*

Golpar – a spice (from Persian hogweed)

Gusht-e kubideh – pounded meat (in *Abgusht* variation, ch.2)

Halva Bushehri (p. 204) – Halva dessert, a sticky sweet

Hamoor – a type of fish

Istikan – small elegant tea glass

Joojeh kabab (p. 105) – Chicken kebab

Joojeh tanoori (p. 96) – Roast poussin

Joojeh za'farani (p. 97) – Saffron lemon chicken

Kabab – kebab, skewered grilled meat

Kaboli polo (p. 146) – Lamb, split peas and raisins rice

Kalam polo Shirazi (p. 149) – Rice with cabbage and fresh herbs

Kateh (p. 130) – a method of cooking rice

Kashk – whey/buttermilk, available in dried or liquid form

Kharbozeh – rock melon

Khiar – small, Middle Eastern cucumber

Khorak – general term for a cooked dish of meat, poultry, fish or vegetables, with less sauce than a khoresht

Khorak-e mahicheh (p. 95) – Lamb shanks in tomato sauce

Khoresht – moist dish of meat, chicken or fish and vegetables, always eaten with rice

Khoresht-e aloo esfenaj (p. 61) – Sweet and sour khoresht with spinach and prunes

Khoresht-e badenjan (p. 65) – Aubergine and lamb khoresht

Khoresht-e bamiyeh (p. 68) – Okra and lamb khoresht

Khoresht-e fesenjan (p. 70) – Chicken khoresht with walnuts and pomegranates

Khoresht-e gharch (p. 72) – Chicken khoresht with saffron and mushrooms

Khoresht-e gheimeh (p. 77) – Lamb khoresht with split peas and fried potatoes

Khoresht-e ghormeh sabzi (p. 79) – Lamb khoresht with red kidney beans and herbs

Khoresht-e karafs (p. 82) – Lamb khoresht with celery and herbs

Khoresht-e seebzamini (p. 85) – Lamb and potato khoresht with tamarind

Koofteh – meatball

Koofteh aloo (p. 107) – Meatballs stuffed with prunes in pomegranate syrup

Koofteh ghelgheli (p. 108) – Miniature meatballs

Koofteh shebet baghala (p. 109) – Dill and broad bean meatballs

Koofteh tarkhoon (p. 111) – Tarragon meatballs

Kookoo (p. 122) – a thick omelette, like a Spanish tortilla

Kotlet (p. 115) – Beef rissoles

Kotlet sibzamini (p. 113) – Potato and meat rissoles

Laboo – beetroot

Lavash – paper-thin Persian flat bread

Limoo amaani – dried limes

Lubia polo (p. 151) – Green beans and lamb rice

Maast – yogurt

Maast va khiar (p. 187) – cucumber and yogurt

Maast-e kisseh – thickened/ strained yogurt

Maast va karafs (p. 184) – celery and yogurt

Maast va laboo (p. 190) – beetroot and yogurt

Mahi ba gashneez (p. 102) – Cod with coriander

Mahi shekampor (p. 100) – Grilled trout with spicy coriander stuffing

Maygoo – prawn

Maygoo polo (p. 153) – Prawns and raisins rice

Morabba va maast (p. 208) – Quince jam and yogurt

Morassa' polo (p. 155) – Saffron jewelled rice (mentioned in Preface, Ch1, Ch3, Ch4)

Morghe shekampor (p. 98) – Roast chicken stuffed with apricot, prune and orange peel

Noghl – sugared almond slivers

Pesteh – pistachio

Polo – a dish of rice mixed with meat, vegetables or fruit

Ranginak (p. 205) – Stuffed dates with walnuts

Rotab – Persian date

Sabzi khordan – fresh herbs served as a side dish

Sabzi polo (p. 159) – Herb rice

Salad-e anar (p. 173) – Pomegranate, cucumber and red onion salad

Salad-e felfel tanoori (p. 174) – Roast pepper salad

Salad-e haft miveh (p. 202) – Seven-fruit salad

Salad-e haveej ba zireh (p. 176) – Carrot and cumin salad

Salad-e ja'fari (p. 175) – Parsley and tomato salad

Salad-e kasni va porteghal (p. 177) – Chicory and orange salad

Salad-e makhloot (p. 179) – Mixed vegetable salad

Salad-e porteghal va ja'fari (p. 178) – Orange and parsley salad with chilli

Salad-e Shirazi (p. 181) – Cucumber, tomato and onion salad

Salad Olivier (p. 191) – Russian salad

Sangak – wholemeal bread made in clay ovens on a bed of hot gravel

Seeb – tart apples

Sekanjabin – sweet and sour syrup as a base for a cold drink (p. 217)

Shalgham – turnip

Sharbat – sweet syrup or cordial

Sharbat-e ablimoo – lime juice drink (p. 216)

Sharbat-e albaloo – sour cherries drink (p. 216)

Sharbat-e golab – rose water drink (p. 218)

Sharbat-e khiar sekanjabin (p. 217) – sweet and sour cucumber drink

Shirin polo = Morassa' polo

Sholleh zard (p. 207) – saffron rice pudding

Shoorba – a thin soup of rice and herbs

Sofreh – elaborate Persian spread (also the name for the cloth on which food is served)

Soup-e joojeh (p. 54) – chicken and fresh coriander soup

Soup-e makhloot (p. 55) – winter vegetable soup

Taaftoon – thin flat bread

Tahchin ghalebi (p. 161) – Saffron, yogurt and chicken 'upside down' rice (sometimes referred to simply as *Tahchin*)

Tahdig – crust from the bottom of the pan in which the rice was cooked

Torsh – 'sour'; also the word for a hot fruit-based drink

Torsh-e albaloo (sour cherries) (p. 214) – hot drink

Torsh-e seeb (sour apples) (p. 214) – hot drink

Torsh-e beh (quince) (p. 215) – hot drink

Torshi – pickles

Zereshk – barberry

Zereshk polo (p. 164) – Saffron barberry rice

Zireh polo (p. 167) – Cumin saffron rice

List of Recipes

Index

The index is in word by word order; photographs are marked in italics e.g.: rose petals *11*